To

MW00927881

Deceived
The Visible Church and the Homosexual Agenda

Dr. David C. Craig, Th.D.

David Craig

12-15-13

II Timothy 3:16-17

Scripture taken from the New King James Version. Copyright © 1982 by Thomas Nelson, Inc. Used by permission. All rights reserved.

ISBN-10: 1490546944
ISBN-13: 978-1490546940

DEDICATION

This book is dedicated to my dear friend and mentor Dr. David Moore. For many years he has rejoiced with me in victories, prayed with me in calamities, encouraged me in ministry and enriched me by his wonderful fellowship. He has been a stalwart of the faith and truth of God and His word and has brought blessings to the many thousands who have come under his shepherd's care.

CONTENTS

ACKNOWLEDGMENTS

I want to give special acknowledgment to Don Thorson for all his help with this book. I sent it to him for an opinion on its content. He is a trusted soldier of the Lord and I wanted to make sure I said what should be said and didn't say what shouldn't. He was kind enough to agree to undertake that task. But, he went above and beyond the call of duty. He edited the book's grammar which was indeed in need of editing. He made sure the message was clear. His help was invaluable. Then he added to his kindness by giving me an endorsement for the book. Such depth and breadth of help is rare. Thank you Don.

CHAPTER ONE

AN EXPERT WITNESS

The world looks for answers in a lot of places. There are advice columnists in the newspaper. From Ann Landers to Miss Manners to Dr. Gott we can get advice on just about any subject that we want. If those choices don't give us what we want we can turn to talk radio or twenty-four hour commentary TV to get the opinions we just need to know. Still not happy? There is the internet where a world of people who want to express themselves are putting out whatever opinions they have to a world seeking an opinion on everything.

If we remain unfulfilled or are still not sure then we can visit our local bookstore where the opinionated are not ashamed to offer counsel on any topic of interest. Gurus hold seminars and for only $500 and a weekend's commitment we can be guided into all truth. There is no end to the onslaught of advice on any topic of our choice.

The problem is that the advice is anything but consistent. One reason is that times change and the opinions of man change with it. What Ann offered as advice in 1960 is not likely to be the advice given by a columnist today. Each generation brings new thoughts and perspectives to the table of culture. We don't want yesterday's answers; we want to be up to date. Grandma is sweet, but she is rather old fashioned after all.

Another reason for inconsistency is perspective. If we were to attend a rally of a conservative political candidate we would hear a different opinion than if we went to the rally of a liberal candidate. They could both address the same issue without providing the same solution. The old adage "consider the source" is important when receiving advice.

Still another reason for inconsistency is the source of authority. Each advice giver may cite a different authority to support their opinion. In the stock market there are both "bull" and "bear" analysts who offer strikingly different advice on what to buy or sell. Their opinions vary depending on whom they support in economic theory. There is certainly no shortage of advice. There is only a shortage of good and consistent advice.

What is needed is an expert witness. We need someone reliable, truthful and knowledgeable. We need advice and wisdom that has proven accurate and consistent over the span of millennia. We need the Bible which is free from the three considerations that make man-made wisdom and advice so inconsistent. The Psalmist 119:89 said, *"Forever, O Lord, thy word is settled in heaven."* It is a timeless word. Isaiah said, *"The grass withers, the flower fades, but the word of God shall stand forever."* (40:8) In Matthew 24:35 Jesus declares, *"Heaven and earth shall pass away, but my words shall not pass away."* The author of Hebrews said of Jesus, *"Jesus Christ, the same yesterday, and today, and forever."* (13:8) The counsel, warnings and teachings of Jesus are as new and relevant today as any day in history. They are forever settled and will not change. We cannot say they are old hat without also calling Jesus old hat.

Perspective was another reason for inconsistency of advice from men. The perspective of the Bible does not have that problem. Peter said, *"Knowing this first that no prophecy of scripture is of any private interpretation. For the prophecy came not in old time by the will of man: but holy men of God spake as they were moved by the Holy Ghost."* (II Peter 1:20-21) While the Bible has multiple human scribes, it has one perspective–God's. Paul wrote, *"All scripture is given by inspiration of God."* (II Timothy 3:16) It all comes from the same source. Whether Moses, David, Isaiah or Paul penned the words on paper, the Bible had come to them from God. It is His consistent perspective we find throughout the whole Bible.

The third reason we find in inconsistent advice is that of cited authority. Behind each opinion there is an expert who guided the opinion giver, and each expert is directed by their own opinion. Such circular reasoning can leave us running in circles or just greatly confused. In economic theory there is no dispute about what the facts are. The facts are there for anyone to read. But since there is no "original source" of interpretation about those facts, different authorities read them differently. Without a foundational authority there can and will be wide diversity of opinion from interpretational authorities.

For some things, like a car or a blender, there can be a more concrete authority. We know that the best authority for manufactured items is the manufacturer. Theirs isn't an opinion; it is fact based on the creative process of the product. They made the product and their ideas on its maintenance and repair comes from a thorough knowledge of the product from the inside out. While we may argue about what kind of car is best, we must acknowledge that the manufacturer of any given model knows more about it than anyone else. We have in the maker, provided he is a person of integrity, a concrete authority. There can be no one with more integrity than God.

The psalmist declared, *"It is he that hath made us and not we ourselves."* (100:3) In God we have a concrete authority about man. David said in Psalm 139:14, *"I will praise thee, for I am fearfully and wonderfully made."* The book of Job declares that God made us. (33:4) Moses declared that God made us. (Genesis 1 and 2) John declared that God made us. (John 1:3) Paul declared that God made us. (Colossians 1:16-17) Jesus declared that God made us. (Matthew 19:4-5) In regard to man, God is the concrete authority. He is the maker. His opinion alone matters in the affairs of men. He is the divine interpreter of His own divinely inspired book.

So, we come to the Bible as the source of our information about all issues of life. We may certainly have our own opinions, but they are really inconsequential. God gives the answer to our assumption about the importance of our thoughts. In Isaiah 55:8-9 God says, *"For my thoughts are not your thoughts, neither are your ways my ways, says the Lord. For as the heavens are higher than the earth, so are my ways higher than your ways, and my thoughts than your thoughts."* Romans 3:4 says *"Let God be true, but every man a liar".* There is an opinion that counts. It is God's.

God has revealed to us in His word what His thoughts are to the extent that we can understand them. He has thoughts that we cannot understand and ways that are past revealing. (Deuteronomy 29:29 and Romans 11:33) Ours is not to speculate what those might be or to be concerned about their day to day implications for man. We are to be concerned about what has been revealed and to do it.

God's word is inspired and it is useful. II Timothy 3:16 and 17 tell of its importance. *"It is profitable for doctrine, for reproof, for correction and for instruction in righteousness."* By it and it alone can the man of God be thoroughly furnished for every good work. It is the word of God that has been given to instruct the church. The true church, Christ's true bride, will accept its statements about its own validity and integrity as inspired by God and therefore true.

Psalm 12:6 says that *"the words of the Lord are pure words".* Psalm 19:7-9 says that the words of the Lord are perfect, sure, right, pure and righteous altogether. In Psalm 19:11 it says that the servant of God is warned by them. Psalm 119:9 says that we will keep our way clean by taking heed to the word of God. Verse 11 of the same psalm says that the word will keep us from sin. Verse 105 of the same psalm tells us that we will be rightly guided in life by the word of God.

It is to the word of God, the Holy Scriptures, to which we shall turn for our instruction regarding the practice of homosexuality and other sexual sin. Since the Bible has been given to the church for our instruction, then it is to the Bible that we will mainly look for our answers regarding church polity on all matters of behavior. What do the consistent words of the Old and New Testaments, given by our Expert Witness and backed by His sole authority, say regarding this issue? That is the foundation, framework and roof for a Biblical response.

CHAPTER TWO

TWO CHURCHES: VISIBLE AND SPIRITUAL

Isn't the visible church the church? Or isn't all the church visible? Certainly the church on the corner is visible. The church on TV is visible. The many internet sites that represent various churches are visible. All that is true. But the Scriptures give a much deeper sense of what the church is. The Scriptures teach that there are actually two entities called "the church". One of these is visible, naked to the eye of every man. The other is a spiritual condition that makes one part of Christ's body, the spiritual and eternal church.

These are not fabricated definitions. The Bible is replete with teaching on the subject of the two churches. We can draw a parallel first from the Biblical teaching about two Israelis. In his letter to the church at Rome Paul said, *"For he is not a Jew which is one outwardly; neither is that circumcision, which is outward in the flesh. But he is a Jew which is one inwardly; and circumcision is that of the heart, in spirit, and not in the letter, whose praise is not of men, but of God."* (Romans 2:28-29) Paul said that in regard to Israel, God draws a distinction between who is and is not a true Jew. A true Israelite is one who approaches God by faith, as Abraham did (Romans 4:3), and not one who strives to be acceptable to God by the law (Romans 10:3). This is the distinction that Paul addressed in the passage in Romans 2.

Jesus addressed the same issue regarding the Jews in John chapter 8. The Jews protested to Jesus in 8:33, *"We are Abraham's seed."* Jesus acknowledged that they were Abraham's seed by the flesh in verse 37, but that they were not Abraham's children. They continued to protest in verse 39 saying, "Abraham is our father." Jesus replied, *"If ye were Abraham's children, ye would do the works of Abraham. But now ye seek to kill me, a man that hath told you the truth, which I have heard of God: this did not Abraham."* (John 8:39-40) Jesus concluded by telling them that they were really of their father the devil. (John 8:44) Jesus made a clear distinction between the visible condition of the flesh and the true condition of the heart.

In fact, Jesus gave multiple warnings to not be confused by appearances. In the Sermon on the Mount, Jesus drew to a close with a comment about appearances and an illustration. First He said that many would come to Him in the Day of Judgment and boast of all the things they had done in His name. These would be people that the world would applaud with recognition for outward manifestation of Christianity. They would, however, receive a chilly response from Christ who will say to them, *"I never knew you: depart from me, ye who work iniquity."* (Matthew 7:21-23)

Then Jesus offered the parable of two houses, one built on rock and one on sand. Jesus Christ is our Rock. The testimony that He is *"the Christ, the Son of the Living God"* (Matthew 16:16) is the rock upon which the church is built. Many build on the sand of good works in Jesus' name. They build on the sand of devotion to an eternal goodness. They build on the sand of the great commandment "love thy neighbor" but deny the truth of the One who gave it. Jesus said that He is the Rock of salvation and that believing on Him is true obedience. (John 3:16) All the houses on sand will fall. (Matthew 7:27) No matter how elaborate the house; no matter how great an expectation of eternal bliss; no matter what sacrifice in life is made; all is for naught if it is not built on the testimony that Jesus Christ is the Son of God. He is the eternally anointed One who came to *"die for our sins, according to the Scriptures, to be buried and raised again the third day, according to the Scriptures"* (I Corinthians 15:3-4) and to be proclaimed as the sole means of man's salvation (Acts 4:12) by faith alone (Ephesians 2:8-9). As the hymnist said, "All other ground is sinking sand." Many will opt for a house on the sand and reject the foundation of Jesus Christ as Lord, the true Son of God. They will not have heard and obeyed, but heard and built their own way. (Matthew 7:24-27)

In this passage Jesus has clearly addressed the issue of the visible and true church. But this is not His only teaching on the subject. In Matthew 13 He gave a series of parables that further illustrate the point. In verses 24-29 Jesus offered the lesson of the wheat and the tares. The good seed was sown in the field by a farmer. While he was sleeping an enemy sowed weed seeds in the same field. When the plants had grown, the weeds were apparent. The servants of the farmer asked if they should tear out the weeds, but were told to wait lest they should also tear out some wheat. At the harvest the weeds and wheat would be separated. The illustration is clear. In the present earthly church there are two groups. One is wheat, useful for the master. One is weeds to be gathered and judged by eternal fire. To the world the wheat and the weeds may look a lot alike, but to the farmer they are different.

In verses 47-50 of Matthew 13 we have a second related parable. Here the picture is of fishing. Jesus had told His disciples, *"Follow me, and I will make you fishers of men."* (Matthew 4:19) Throughout the history of the church fishing has taken place and a great net of fish has been drawn in. All the netted fish have been placed together in the hold of the boat, but later the good fish and the worthless fish will be separated. Jesus pointed out that this is true of the end of the age when the angels shall gather the worthless from the good and cast the worthless into everlasting fire. The visible and the true church are left to mingle together in this life, but the day is coming when God will make a righteous separation.

Clearly Jesus has given repeated teachings regarding the nature of two churches present in the world today. These two churches are not identified by denominational signs on the door. They are not identified by the prominence or insignificance of their buildings, property or programs. They cannot be distinguished by the dress codes used or ignored in any given place of fellowship. They cannot be told apart by the educational achievements of their clergy or their form of church government. Members of the true and visible church mingle together in the pews of many churches in many denominations.

What does distinguish the true from the visible is what each one does with Jesus, the Gospel of Christ and the Word of God. Is Jesus Christ exalted as the eternal God, God the Son of the eternal trinity? If He is exalted as the true Son of God, then His teachings will be believed as true. If not, they will not. The apostle John did battle with the Gnostics on the issue of the doctrine of Christ and His full deity and humanity. In the book of First John chapter 2:22 he said, *"Who is a liar but he that denies that Jesus is the Christ? He is antichrist that denies the Father and the Son."* Peter called these false teachers introducers of *"damnable heresies".* (II Peter 2:1) People who deny the teaching of the Son deny the teaching of the Father and are none of His.

What kind of Gospel is a person presenting? The Gospel is that Christ died for our sins. We are saved through faith in His finished work on the cross for us. Paul said that if any comes with any other gospel than this, *"let him be accursed."* (Galatians 1:8-9) Even in the days of the early church there were false teachers who had gone out to subvert the true gospel. They taught that while faith was good, it was works of the law that really saved a person. Paul spent the entire book of Galatians defending the doctrine of justification by faith alone. The first church synod held in Jerusalem and found in Acts 15 upheld this doctrine. Acts 15:9 and 11 say, *"And [God] put no difference between us and them, purifying their hearts by faith. But we believe that through the grace of the Lord Jesus Christ, shall we be saved, even as they* [those who had come to faith without regard to Jewish ceremonial law]".

A false Christ and a false gospel are two evidences of those who are part of the visible but not the true church. A third is what they do with the Word of God. They will be like the serpent in the Garden of Eden. His approach to Eve began with this question, *"Hath God said?"* (Genesis 3:1) That is the first approach taken by the false teacher. "Did God really say that?" But that is just the beginning. Eve told the serpent that if they ate or *touched* (her addition) the fruit, they would die. The serpent then moved beyond questioning to outright lying by saying, *"Ye shall not surely die."* From the fall of man to this day, the mark of the false teacher is to ask if God really said what He said, and then to deny that God meant what He said.

One key way that false teachers will deny the Word is by introducing license to sin freely. Jude warned in verse 4 of his book, *"For there are certain men crept in unawares, who were before of old ordained to this condemnation, ungodly men, turning the grace of our God into lasciviousness, and denying the only Lord God and our Lord Jesus Christ."* False teachers will deny God's complete holiness which he has declared of Himself *"for I the Lord your God am holy"* (Leviticus 19:1) They will also deny that God's rules are relevant for our lives and either exempt or excuse away behaviors that lead us to break His demand, *"Ye shall be holy."* Leviticus 19:1

The visible church may say, they may indeed protest loudly, that they believe in God. They may name the name of Jesus Christ and carry their Bibles and even quote from them, but Jesus has already issued the warning, *"I never knew you: depart from me, ye who work iniquity."* (Matthew 7:21-23) If they teach the wrong Christ, preach the wrong gospel and question the authority of God's Word, they are under God's judgment already. The visible church and true church abide today side by side. It is the visible church, corrupted by the unregenerate, who have embraced the false teachings of man on many issues. Homosexual behavior is one of them.

CHAPTER THREE

IS IT REALLY AN ISSUE?

Is lascivious teaching from the pulpit really an issue? To clarify that question, would a pastor really stand in the pulpit and promote an act or behavior that the Bible has clearly revealed to be lewd, sexually impure or wanton in the context of spiritual morality? Would someone in a position of biblical authority such as: a pastor, a bishop, a synod, a denomination or a rightly constituted board of elders or deacons really advocate for immoral behavior? The answer to that question is a sad but resounding – "YES". Thankfully God has preserved His true church where the answer would be no, but the visible church gives a different response.

This is not new. Jude warned of it in verse 4 of his short epistle. *"For there are certain men crept in unawares, who were before of old ordained to this condemnation, ungodly men, turning the grace of our God into lasciviousness, and denying the only Lord God and our Lord Jesus Christ."* These men had become important enough in the early church to have been able to turn the message from holiness to a holy God into lasciviousness for an indifferent god.

Paul in his second letter to Timothy mentioned a similar situation. The last days of waiting for the return of Christ had officially begun when He ascended into heaven and the angels gave the pronouncement that He would come again in like manner. At that point the clock of the last days began to tick. Paul warned in II Timothy 3:1, *"in the last days perilous times shall come."* In verse 3 he added that people would live in those days *"Without natural affection."* Then in verse 6 he acknowledged that such things had already begun.

In II Corinthians 12:21 Paul told the church of Corinth that they had been lax in dealing with the sin of lasciviousness. The leaders of the church it seemed would rather have ignored it than taken a stand on it. Paul assured them that he would take a stand on the issue when he came again to Corinth. Silence from the pulpit on the issue of lascivious behavior is equal to open consent to it.

But the problem is older than New Testament churches. The Old Testament prophets of God were often in conflict with the false prophets of their day. Jeremiah had great problems with the false prophets. In Jeremiah 23:9-11 we read, *"My heart within me is broken because of the prophets; all my bones shake. I am like a drunken man, and like a man whom wine has overcome, because of the LORD, and because of His holy words. For the land is full of adulterers; for because of a curse the land mourns. The pleasant places of the wilderness are dried up. Their course of life is evil, and their might is not right. For both prophet and priest are profane; yes, in My house I have found their wickedness, says the LORD."* In verse 14 it goes on and says, *"Also I have seen a horrible thing in the prophets of Jerusalem: they commit adultery and walk in lies; they also strengthen the hands of evildoers, so that no one turns back from his wickedness. All of them are like Sodom to Me, and her inhabitants like Gomorrah."* Lascivious tolerance and lascivious actions by people of ecclesiastical leadership undermine the integrity of God's holiness in this world.

The problem of quietly condoning immorality or openly proclaiming it and even having leaders openly practice it goes back to the earliest days of the church and Old Testament false prophets. So, yes, it is an issue that needs to be addressed. Paul addressed it. Jude addressed it. Peter addressed it by saying that it was enough to have lived that way before we got saved, but now that was to no longer be true of our lives. (I Peter 4:3) The church today needs to address the issue of immoral, lascivious behavior with the full force of biblical authority.

Unfortunately the visible church is destroying the public perception of biblical authority. Whole denominations are voting to accept immoral behavior, specifically homosexuality, as God-accepted behavior. Every two years the issue comes before the general assembly of the United Presbyterian Church (PCUSA) at their General Assembly[1] and is gladly reported in the public press. In recent years the Episcopal Church in America has openly ordained a homosexual bishop[2]. The Evangelical Lutheran Church in America (ELCA) has granted privilege of pastorate to openly gay men and women[3]. The United Church of Christ (UCC) has openly announced itself as an embracing denomination[4]. The Reformed Church in America (RCA), while still outwardly maintaining a position of opposition to homosexual clergy and homosexual marriage in general, is still having an ongoing dialog on the issue and accepts credentials with the PCUSA, ELCA and the UCC[5]. In 2010 the RCA adopted the Belhar Confession as its fourth standard of unity. The drafter of this confession openly asserts the document calls for the acceptance and the ordination of homosexuals[6]. The essence of the position of these denominations seems to be that God is not concerned about how we live, just that we "love" him (or her as in the case of new liturgies)[7].

These denominations are not very large ones. Their total membership according to their own denominational web sites from 2006-2007 is about 10 million people. According to Wikipedia the membership for the Southern Baptist Church alone is over 16,000,000. That is larger than the five other denominations combined. Also according to Wikipedia there are over 68,000,000 members of the Roman Catholic Church in the United States. That is almost seven times the number in the above named five denominations. Yet, despite their size, the stand being taken by these four denominations (the RCA excluded) is so consistent with the world's position on accepting lascivious behavior that their actions are fully reported and distorted beyond the influence these denominations actually possess.

The perception is created that maybe God does not really care about immoral behavior. I hear it from the members of my own church. Are we wrong? Are they right? If what you (our pastor) are saying comes from the Bible, why does it disagree with what others are saying? Across America the question is being pushed harder and harder against the vast majority of American believers who oppose immorality. They challenge the church, "Why are you so callously and hard-heartedly against the loving stance that these major denominations take?" Like the false prophets of Jeremiah's day they are creating a world comfortable with an unreal and uncaring God.

In November of 2006, Oliver Thomas wrote an article for the op-ed page of the *USA Today* newspaper. Mr. Thomas's article was entitled "When religion loses its credibility[8]." This article purports to come from a religious man who is speaking on behalf of a god who has been totally misrepresented by the religious establishment. That he is not speaking for the God of the Bible will be laid out in the coming chapters. The point is that he says that he is speaking for that God and he, along with the fellow sufferers for truth that agree with him, is the only one who has gotten it right. When the church will get honest and speak God's truth as he claims to be doing, then all will be well in "Religionville" again.

Of course *USA Today* is a secular publication and is only too willing to print such worldly opinions. The article was first brought to my attention by a church member who wanted to know if it was correct. The big lie has been told over and over and over again. The people in the pews are beginning to wonder what is going on. These are not unintelligent people. They are not slackers in their faithful religious practice. They are the average person who simply hears the same song over and over again until they cannot get it out of their head.

What are the lies that are repeated over and over again in our society that are so strongly affecting our churches? Lie one: homosexuality is normal. Lie two: homosexuality is an inborn trait. Lie three: homosexuality is not condemned by God. Lie four: (based on lie three) Only a few cultural bigots from ancient times wrote homophobic things in the Bible, but those passages are only the opinion of those few bigoted men. Lie five: If you don't believe and give in to lies one through four then you are a homophobic bigot and need another course in diversity training and then another one until you do agree and give in. They seem to say, in fact, that the entire moving forward of society is imperiled by the bigotry of those who oppose their position.

Will the presentation of the truth change the minds of those who hold to these lies? Probably not. Did Jeremiah's preaching convert the false prophets? No, it did not. Micaiah's prophecy in I Kings 22 against the false prophets did not stop their false prophecy. Did Elijah's victory over the false prophets of Baal stop others from taking their place as servants in the temples of those false gods? No, it did not. Did Amos' prophecy against Amaziah (Amos 6:10-17) bring repentance from Amaziah? No, it did not. Will the teachings of these lessons bring sweeping spiritual change to Mr. Thomas and the homosexual community? No, probably not.

That does not mean that the prophets of old and the writers of the New Testament were wasting their breath when they spoke and wrote the words of God. Jesus said, *"My sheep hear my voice and I know them and they follow me."* (John 10:27) Bible lessons are for the sheep of Christ. His sheep need to know clearly, concisely and completely what He has to say to them. When they hear the words of truth they will discern them and understand the righteousness of God. It is insufficient to say,

"The Bible condemns homosexuality" and then to add, "God will judge them all." The issues that are raised need to be fully answered. If we can't answer them then people will assume that there are no answers or that we are hiding something and don't want to tell. In either case it is a ripe opportunity for the world to continue with the big lie system and for the untaught believer to become more confused. God has answers. His word is full of them. When it comes to sin He has a lot to say. He exposes the root of sin, the course of sin, the life consequence of sin and the eternal condemnation of sin. There is no part of the big lie that He has not answered in His word. We need to hear the voice of Christ calling to us from its pages and rejoice in the comforting truth of that voice. The church needs the honest answers and full explanation of God's view on homosexuality. We will look at them all.

CHAPTER FOUR

CHANGE THAT TUNE?

Mr. Thomas is a lawyer. I don't mention that to denigrate him or cause instant antagonism against his profession. I happen to know some lawyers and think highly of them all. I mention it because of how he will argue his case against biblical interpretation of the scriptures in general and those opposed to his point of view. It is the art of misdirection.

I once sat on a jury. The defendant had been caught red handed with six packages of crack cocaine, two large guns, a small scale for weighing drugs and a package of baggies used for packing the drugs for resale. It seemed like a slam dunk open and shut case. Apparently the county attorney and the police thought so too, but it didn't turn out that neatly. There were two reasons, both related to the challenge homosexuals are making against the truth of the Word of God.

The defense attorney did not have to prove her client innocent. In America the defendant is innocent until proven guilty. There was no disputing the evidence against the client. The police had videotaped the arrest, the seizure of the guns, the scale and the baggies. There were six credible eye witnesses that the defendant had six bags of crack cocaine in his mouth at the time of the arrest. He had fled the scene in the process of the search and had to be subdued by a police dog and a taser.

Still he resisted arrest. Those were the facts that were undisputed. He was charged with three crimes: possession of a controlled substance, intent to deliver a controlled substance and possession of a firearm in the act of delivering a controlled substance.

The first witness was the primary arresting officer. There were actually either six or eight officers involved in the arrest by the time it was all done. The first question from the defense was simple, "What direction was the defendant driving when you began to follow him?" I thought it was an absurd question. Based on already given evidence he was driving toward the river and everyone in town knows that is south. Everyone, it seems, except the arresting officer. He answered, "North." Oops! "Are you sure?" queried the defense. "Pretty sure. I am directionally challenged," replied the officer. Oops again!

Which way the defendant was driving was entirely irrelevant to the case. We had a video tape of the pursuit and arrest. It seemed so meaningless and a waste of taxpayer money to pay jurors to hear an irrelevant question. I was wrong!

The next witness was a rookie officer. He was still on probation as a new officer. He had been in the pursuit vehicle as well and was the second primary arresting officer. "Where were you standing while the other officer approached the vehicle?" He answered without wavering a second, "I was standing by the rear taillight of the driver's side." I can't remember where I was for half of yesterday so I was impressed by his response. He was wrong, of course. He was actually standing closer to the side gas tank than the rear taillight. Oops! Again, who cared? It was a matter of two feet and didn't change the facts.

But it did matter. The avalanche of misdirection continued. The defendant was no longer on trial. The police were now on trial. The misdirection had taken place very smoothly. The focus was off the sin and on the accuser. How well did this tactic work? The accused was found not guilty of any crime other than possession. Instead of twenty-five years in prison it was probably probation. It never even made it into the newspaper. Misdirection is one of the two factors in deciding the case. The other we will deal with later.

Misdirection is a great legal tactic and Mr. Thomas uses it with great ease in his case against biblical truth. The defendant, homosexuality, is not on trial. The accusers who assert that homosexuality is a sin are on trial. He has changed the tune, reframed the argument and can quietly slip away from guilt. It is so easy to lose track of what is being discussed.

Is there a biblical response to misdirection? There may not be a direct biblical response. But there is a response that is biblical. The misdirection pointed the finger at the accuser instead of the accused. A biblical response begins with honesty. Yes, we are human and we make mistakes. Mr. Thomas begins his misdirection with the statement, "Galileo was persecuted for revealing what we now know to be truth regarding earth's place in our solar system." Then he likens the persecution of Galileo to homosexuals and asks, "Will Christian leaders once again be on the wrong side of history?"[1]

There it is in black and white. The accusation is made. You, the church, were wrong once, so you must be untrustworthy and wrong again. The wrongness of the past must be a complete and linear wrongness. You have never stopped being wrong. You did not do due diligence when it came to Galileo, so you must not be doing due diligence today. Misdirection just changed the argument. The church's past is in error so her present cannot be trusted.

How do we respond to the issue? Do we say, "Well, we are not Catholics so this charge does not apply to us." That leaves the charge still hanging there. We could say, "Well, the Catholics persecuted the Protestants as well, so big deal about Galileo." That doesn't help as the charge is still out there. The charge is that the church is in error. The second response only proves the error to be correct. If we follow this line of argument we get headed down a road that diverts from the issue of homosexuality and falls into an impossible trap of historical justification. We cannot justify history.

That is the key point. We cannot justify human history. We cannot justify church history. We cannot justify our own personal history. We began in sin and error of our ways. The solution to that was confession and repentance and calling upon Christ for salvation. That becomes the basis for our response to the accusation of our past error.

Paul gave us the right response in I Corinthians 6:11. *"And such were some of you: but ye are washed, but ye are sanctified, but ye are justified in the name of the Lord Jesus and by the Spirit of our God."* Our answer is, "We have sinned and acted immorally (for certainly persecution is an immoral act) but God has forgiven the sin, cleansed our hearts and instructed us in truth. That truth includes the admission of our own sinfulness and that our only right declaration about sin is the clear teaching given to us by the Spirit of God." Now we can declare the truth since we are back on track. We are not on trial any longer; the focus is back on the sin. Now we do not stand on self-justification or failed historical justification; we stand on the truth of the Word of God. We are preparing to give a biblical response.

But Mr. Thomas is not quite done with this issue just yet. He takes up a second strand of misdirection and reveals the second reason the defendant got off so easily on the drug charge. Thomas cites three examples of the church being unfair or condemning homosexual behavior and then asks, "What if we're wrong?" He keeps the reframing of the issue alive by the use of the word "we" in context of who is wrong on the issue of homosexuality. By the use of the word "we" he is implying that he is speaking on behalf of the Christian community. That is largely like Judas saying that he spoke on behalf of the other eleven disciples or of Christ.

Who speaks for the Christian community? A person I knew went off to seminary, a "supposed" Christian community. He believed in the inerrant Scriptures, the virgin birth of Christ and the other key fundamentals of faith as laid out by R. A. Torrey in his composite work The Fundamentals in 1909. His first contact at the seminary was with a school official who knew the state from which he came and the position that the churches of that state took on those issues. That official told him in a very straightforward statement, "To survive in this school you will have to change your ways and your position." While earning high marks in all of his classes during the coming school year this person was asked at the end of the year to finish his education elsewhere. He had not and would not change. That seminary official spoke for the visible church, but not for Christ. Mr. Thomas wants us to believe that he is part of and speaking for the Christian community. He wants us to believe that he has our best interest at stake. The use of the word "we" continues his misdirection of the facts.

On our jury was a woman who had clearly misrepresented the facts when she went through the process of jury screening. We were all asked if we had any knowledge of drugs or drug related issues. She emphatically stated that she did not. During jury deliberations, however, she demonstrated that to have been a great "half-truth". She had never used drugs, but she knew people that did. She repeatedly used her street knowledge of drugs to criticize the testimony of the expert witnesses called by the prosecution. She was, as Jude pointed out in his book, one who had crept in unawares and teaches a contrary doctrine. Her presence in the jury room amplified the effect of the misdirection offered by the defense. Misdirection coupled with misrepresentation of the truth changed the outcome of the verdict.

Mr. Thomas uses both misdirection and misrepresentation to change the tune of the issue at hand. The issue is not the sin of the church, past or present. It is the sin that the Word of God exposes. Secondly, those who do not speak for the truth of the Word of God do not speak for the true church. Satan twisted the Word of God toward Eve in the Garden while pretending to have her best interest at heart. He was not on her side and Mr. Thomas is not on the side of the spiritual church. He cannot propose to speak for the church no matter how often he wants to misdirect or misrepresent the truth by seeming to do so. Misdirection and misrepresentation must be answered from a biblical perspective.

CHAPTER FIVE

BY WHOSE LOGIC?

What captivates me most about the article by Mr. Thomas is the well rounded appearance of those who are involved in the attack on the church and biblical teaching. According to the web site for the First Amendment Center[1], and according to the article printed in *USA Today*[2], Mr. Thomas is not only a lawyer but also a minister. According to the above web site Mr. Thomas has argued cases at all levels of the court system including the United States Supreme Court. He is considered to be a respected authority on constitutional matters. He also taught at Georgetown University Law Center and is (was) an elected member of his local school board. He represents the voices of both the visible church and state. In addition to this he writes regularly for *USA Today* and therefore also represents the voice of American media. The man is no slouch. He is a knowledgeable, respected and articulate spokesman for the visible church, the government and public opinion.

Psalm 2:2-3 says, *"The kings of the earth set themselves, and the rulers take counsel together, against the LORD and against his anointed, saying, Let us break their bands asunder, and cast away their cords from us."* Mr. Thomas represents the "kings of the earth", both legal and public, as well as the "rulers" who were the religious rulers of the people. While we say that there is a separation of church

24

and state, that is not entirely correct. There cannot be a complete separation of church and state because Satan is the god of this world (II Corinthians 4:4). Daniel chapter 10 verses 12-20 clearly teach the involvement of demonic spiritual forces in the governments of man. Jesus said that the opinions of the unsaved members of the visible church are the opinions of Satan (John 8:39-45). Therefore we find the opinions of the unsaved members of the visible church readily offered by the kings of the earth who are also under his authority. The unsaved members of the visible church and the state are therefore not separate and the state and public opinion then naturally gravitate together. Therefore we find the words of Psalm 2:2-3 continuing to play out in the world today against the truth of Jesus Christ and His word as it played out against Christ Himself when he was on earth. The article by Mr. Thomas represents the combined voices of opposition to Christ encapsulated into one neat package.

What is the purpose of the combined opinions of unbiblical man? It is to cast off the restraints of God as stated in Psalm 2:3. It is to end the reign of obedience to the Father's will as Satan deceived Eve into doing in the Garden of Eden. It is to make man god and God irrelevant. This is not just the work of Mr. Thomas, it is the work of all who reject the authority of God and thus fall under the authority of Satan since he began his work of cultivating rebellion in our first parents.

The thing is that they say it so articulately. They have so many platforms from which to declare their rebellion that the message cannot be ignored. Media, business, government and education all combine to offer a message contrary to God's message. There is a constant emphasis on "our rights" or "our worth" which mostly just means that we are the center of everything. If we are the hub around which the world turns, then God isn't. He is diminished to being beneath us. What we think is more important than what He thinks. In fact, our thoughts must be superior to His since He is of less value than we are. Our reasoning is superior reasoning because it meets our needs. What doesn't meet our needs is of necessity wrong since we have so much value, worth and possess so many inherent rights.

This is the logic of the age. Logic of past ages has stated that the state is supreme or the king is supreme. It was necessary for the survival of a given civilization to submit all to that given authority and abandon self. That logic was also flawed. It still made man the center of all things even if the individual man wasn't. It misses the biblical logic of all creation as stated in Revelation 4:11, *"Thou art worthy, O Lord, to receive glory and honor and power: for thou hast created all things and for Thy pleasure they are and were created."*

This introduces a divine reason "to be" that defies human logic. It is, unfortunately, a divine reason to be that is poorly articulated from vastly too many pulpits and in too few Christian lives. Mr. Thomas states his thinking concisely, neatly and clearly. The ax bites deepest that is most sharply honed. It is incumbent upon the church to be skilled in the Word of God. Paul admonished the believer, *"Study to show thyself approved unto God, a workman that needs not to be ashamed, rightly dividing the word of truth."* (II Timothy 2:15)

Paul told us that our defensive and our offensive weapons of argument are to be the Word of God. It is not with human arguments that we are to prevail in spiritual matters. The wisdom of men will perish, but the Word of God will stand forever. Paul told us the fate of man's wisdom in I Corinthians 1:19 *"For it is written, 'I will destroy the wisdom of the wise, and will bring to nothing the understanding of the prudent."* Paul then asked, *"Where is the wise? Where is the disputer (debater) of this world? Hath not God made foolish the wisdom of this world?"* While I wish to be as articulate as Mr. Thomas, a goal but probably not a reality, I wish to do so with truth that endures. God speaks in Isaiah 40:8, *"The grass withers, the flower fades: but the word of our God shall stand forever."*

Mr. Thomas can present the opinions of the world view, including the unsaved visible church view, as clearly as anyone. His ax of logic and debate are highly honed. Like the grass, however, his views will fade and then be burned. It is a different view that must be used to present the truth. Jesus prayed in John 17:17, *"Sanctify them through thy truth: Thy word is truth."* In Luke 11 Jesus teaches that when we are confronted for His sake that it is the Spirit who is to give us the answer. It is the Spirit that spoke the Scriptures to the prophets and apostles. Peter recorded it in II Peter 1:20-21, *"Knowing first that no prophecy of the scripture is of any private interpretation. For the prophecy came not in old time by the will of man: but holy men of God spake as they were moved by the Holy Ghost."*

It is spiritual reasoning that must be applied to all matters of faith and practice for the Holy Spirit is to be our guide in all matters of faith and practice. We need His guidance because we don't think or reason correctly on our own. Our own view is tarnished by sin. It is God's view that we need. God put it this way in Isaiah 55:8-9, *"For my thoughts are not your thoughts, neither are your ways my ways, says the LORD. For as the heavens are higher than the earth, so are my ways higher than your ways, and my thoughts than your thoughts."* If we are going to reason for God, then we need to reason by the Word of God.

This reasoning is not guaranteed to hit a home run in the world. It is divine reason and it is contrary to the will and heart of men. Paul said that we have not received the spirit of the world (I Corinthians 2:12) but we have received the Spirit of God. Galatians 5 outlines the conflict between the spirit of man (flesh) and Spirit of God. We began this life with the spirit of man being born in human nature by the will of man. We are born again, become part of the true church, by the working of the Holy Spirit. (John 3:3-6) We do not then receive again the spirit of man because we already have it and it is condemned forever. We do receive the Holy Spirit who is eternal and gives us eternal life. This Spirit of God now leads us in a new direction. He gives us new focus and a new outlook. He removes our false view of self as supreme and reveals to us and in us that God is supreme. But there is a problem here. The world does not possess the Spirit of God.

The world does not receive the things of God as a logical conclusion. Paul explained the situation in I Corinthians 2:14. *"But the natural man receives not the things of the Spirit of God: for they are foolishness unto him: neither can he know them because they are spiritually discerned."* The thinking of God draws more of a blank stare from the world than it does loud applause. That doesn't mean that the presentation of truth is a failure because it doesn't hit that grand slam we so hope that it will. It will still accomplish His will. In some cases that will be vindication in judgment. When God righteously judges the world, each man's response to His revelation will reveal the righteousness of that judgment. To those who believe it is eternal life. To those who don't believe it will produce righteous judgment for not believing Him to be true. God likens His word to rain that comes down from heaven and waters the earth producing fruit. (Isaiah 55:9) Then He says, *"So shall my word be that goes forth out of my mouth: it shall not return unto me void, but it shall accomplish that which I please, and it shall prosper in the thing whereto I sent it."* (Isaiah 55:10)

Mr. Thomas can reason well from the view of man. He has the world's point of view quite clearly explained. But since he has chosen to take on God's point of view and argue with thoughts higher than his thoughts, then a biblical response is necessary. It is also necessary so that the true church can be grounded in the truth of God's Word. It is important to know clearly what it says and have confident peace that there will be a righteous vindication for them and for their faith and for their practice of faith. They can know there is a righteous condemnation for those who publicly mock them and mock God's Word. Paul shared God's promise that just such an end will occur in II Thessalonians 5:6, *"Seeing it is a righteous thing with*

God to recompense tribulation to them that trouble you." It is not that we seek judgment for others. We seek their repentance and salvation. But God is the ultimate and supreme Judge and we can be confident that we will leave the eternal courtroom satisfied with His decree.

CHAPTER SIX

IS IT REALLY OUR PRIMARY POSITION?

Mr. Thomas begins his attack on Christian opposition to homosexuality with a bold assertion. He says, "[Their main reason for] persisting in their view that homosexuality is wrong...is found in Leviticus 18, *You shall not lie with a man as with a woman; it is an abomination*'.[1]" This verse is found in Leviticus 18:22. He holds forth this argument since he tries to annul any value of Leviticus 18 to the church in the modern age. While the value of Leviticus is another issue entirely, is this one verse in Leviticus really the only Old Testament leg the church can stand on to oppose homosexual conduct. Indeed, is it the primary text that we would use?

This approach is called "shortening the field". If Mr. Thomas and others want to diminish the Bible's opposition to homosexuality, then they must shorten the field. They must eliminate or devalue any other arguments or biblical points that the believer may use. This argument is great to use in a worldly context where few have any biblical knowledge. The response of the world is something like this, "Well, if that is their only argument and since you say that Leviticus is irrelevant anyway, well, then I guess the Bible really doesn't oppose homosexuality at all." The goal of shortening the field is successful if the audience doesn't know anything about the rules of the game.

This leads to another, and sadder, situation. According to a Pew Research Poll conducted in the summer of 2010 and published by the *Los Angeles Times* on September 28, 2010, Mr. Thomas will be as equally successful in using his shortening the field technique with church members as with the unchurched general public. The article is entitled "Atheists, agnostics most knowledgeable about religion, survey finds.[2]" It draws sad conclusions regarding the great sea of general ignorance that passes for contemporary Christianity.

According to a related Gallup Poll taken in October of 2000 only 16% of all Americans claim to read their Bibles daily. That information is now 10 years old. That poll noted that from 1980 to 1990 the number of readers had declined and had declined again from 1990 to 2000[3]. If nobody in the stands knows the rules of the game, then shortening the field is a great idea. Ocean front property in Arizona is always available for the ignorant. Americans can be handed any religious hogwash and accept it as a new flavor of soda. A biblical response for the true church is necessary and clear and complete biblical teaching is necessary from the pulpits of those who claim true faith in God.

While Moses is credited by Jesus as the author of the first five books of the Old Testament, Leviticus isn't the first book he wrote. If we want to find biblical opposition to homosexual behavior, then we want to begin at the beginning. Moses recorded God's words in Genesis 2:18, *"And the Lord God said, 'It is not good that man should be alone; I will make a help meet (suitable) for him'."* And what kind of suitable mate did God make? *"Then the rib which the Lord God had taken from man He made into a woman, and brought her to the man."* (vs. 22) God made a woman for a man as a suitable mate. That is the start of the story. Long before Moses is told to record God's law against homosexuality, God told us why such a law was a reasonable thing.

Homosexuality also defied another Genesis declaration of God. God, having made man and woman, said, *"Be fruitful and multiply."* (Genesis 1:28) This commandment to be fruitful and multiply cannot be fulfilled in a homosexual union. Such a union defies God's order and commandment. (Here it may help to point out that in Hebrew narrative writing the outline is often given first and then the full narrative is given. This is seen in the order of things in Genesis 1 and 2, 4 and 5, 10 and 11 and elsewhere. The outline of man's creation is given to us in Genesis 1 along with the commandment to be fruitful, and then in Genesis 2 we are given the narrative details of Genesis 1. It is not a biblical flaw to find this order of things; it is ancient narrative style.)

Mr. Thomas would like to ignore these passages and their relevance to the discussion by shortening the field. The reality is that we cannot ignore the completeness of God's word and be fully honest and truthful at the same time. The Old Testament dialogue on homosexuality does not begin in Leviticus, it begins in Genesis.

Proceeding through Genesis we come to one of the most well-known accounts in the Bible. Even if every detail is not known to everyone, the general teaching is understood that God destroyed Sodom and Gomorrah. People of biblical ignorance still have heard of Lot's wife and of the pillar of salt. They are common idioms of our language. Why did God destroy them? Genesis 18:20 says, *"Because the cry of Sodom and Gomorrah is great, and because their sin is grievous."*

Certainly Sodom and Gomorrah had many sins. It is interesting that they are not all listed. In fact, the one that is listed is sexual immorality – specifically homosexuality. Genesis 19:5 says, *"And they* [the men of the city – vs. 4] *called unto Lot, and said unto him, 'Where are the men which came in to thee this night? Bring them out unto us, that we may know them."* Some may say they simply wanted a little get acquainted session, but they should read on. Lot responds, (vs. 7) *"I pray you brethren, do not so wickedly."* If the intent was innocent then no charge of wickedness need be made. Lot continues, (vs. 8) *"Behold now, I have two daughters which have not known a man; let me, I pray you, bring them out unto you, and do ye to them as is good in your eyes; only unto these men do nothing."*

Notice the word "know" in verse 5 and the word "known" in verse 8. No one can escape the context of the statements. The men of Sodom wanted to know sexually the two guests in Lot's house. The men of the city were not some kind of community welcoming committee; they were seeking homosexual contact with the two men (angels) who had come to Lot's house. These men were insistent in their purpose. They did not want Lot's daughters. They wanted the men for sexual purposes. They tried to break into the house and were only stopped from their intent by intervention of the angels. The angels could now fulfill their mission of destroying the city and delivering Lot safely from that destruction.

The sin of Sodom has such long standing impact that its very name is still used as the definition of homosexual behavior. "The term *sodomy* refers to the homosexual activities of men in the story of the city of Sodom in the Bible. The destruction of Sodom and Gomorrah because of their residents' immorality became a central part of Western attitudes toward forms of non-procreative sexual activity and same-sex relations.[4]" It is clear that the record we find in Genesis casts a long shadow down to the time when Leviticus was written. In Genesis God illustrates the rule that He would declare in the Law. It is not an obscure law in seldom read book; that is the point. The point is the whole thing. The whole is the sum of the parts and not just a part that is called the sum.

It must be noted here that in later Old Testament books God does spell out other sins of Sodom not detailed in Genesis. Ezekiel 16:49-50 says, *"Behold, this was the iniquity of thy sister Sodom, pride, fullness of bread, and abundance of idleness was in her and in her daughters, neither did she strengthen the hand of the poor and needy. And they were haughty, and committed abomination before me: therefore I took them away as I saw good."* Those who do not oppose homosexuality will use only the first part of this passage in Ezekiel to defend their position that God's anger was not directly opposed to their sexual practice. But God wrote the whole verse and definitely includes the abomination of homosexuality in it.

As stated earlier Sodom had many sins. In Genesis, when Sodom was destroyed, only one of them is mentioned. In Ezekiel God said that Sodom had committed abomination. He adds that word abomination after the other sins listed. It isn't a summation of the other sins; it is a separate action and needs to be understood as one of the reasons for their destruction. If it were the only reason for their destruction then only homosexuals would need to fear the judgment of God. That is not the case. God marks all sin. In this marking of all sin, homosexuality is on His list. We cannot deflect the judgment of God away from homosexuality and onto the other sins as if the first were OK and the others wrong. All collectively are wrong. All are listed as sins.

There is a twofold problem to address quickly. While homosexuals want to reclassify their behavior as normal and not sinful, the church of today has overstated its case as well. Homosexuals want to believe the lie that sin isn't sin. The church wants to grandstand a particular sin as the most egregious of them all. God does not grant either community the right to rewrite His word. Homosexuality is a sin before God. Genesis, Leviticus and Ezekiel make that plain. Homosexuality is not the only sin before God, however, and it will do the church well to be honest about how God feels about them all. The wages of sin is death. That is all sin and the very nature of sin. Christ, however, died for all sins and the nature of sin. In Him we can have forgiveness and everlasting life. All sinners need to be brought to the cross and homosexuals shouldn't try to avoid coming because they want to rewrite the Book.

CHAPTER SEVEN

SING AN OLD SONG

Is doctrine important? I truly wish that I had $5 for each and every time a congregant of mine or some other church member foolishly said to me, "I really don't care to hear sermons on doctrine. After all, shouldn't we all just get along in Jesus?" First, I would have a huge retirement account and could look forward to some truly golden "golden years". Secondly, I would be justly compensated for having held in so many holy explosions that needed to be let out.

The multiple errors presented in Mr. Thomas' article are most likely to be believed by those who so ignorantly say, "I don't really care to hear doctrinal sermons." Paul expressly warned Timothy about this exact danger when he explained why there is both law and doctrine in I Timothy 1:9-10. *"Knowing this: that the law is not made for a righteous person, but for the lawless and insubordinate, for the ungodly and for sinners, for the unholy and profane, for murderers of fathers and murderers of mothers, for manslayers, for fornicators, for sodomites, for kidnappers, for liars, for perjurers, and if there is any other thing that is contrary **to sound doctrine**."*

In Acts 2:42 Luke recorded that the early believers were actually devoted to doctrine: *"And they continued steadfastly in the **apostles' doctrine** and fellowship, and in breaking of bread, and in* *prayers."*

Those who are devoted to doctrine, not just the kind that differentiates one small group of believers from another, but the kind that upholds the doctrines of Christ and the apostles, are armed for spiritual warfare and the attacks against the substance of faith in Christ. Doctrine is just an English translation of the Greek word "teaching" and it is the teachings of Christ that are under attack by the comments of Mr. Thomas and so many others who advocate a new or redefined position on God and godliness.

This brings us to an argument that Mr. Thomas does not make, but is essential to the next one he will make. What is the true identity of all mankind? Are we, the whole world community today, still in the same condition of being made "in the image of God" that Adam and Eve were in? This verse from Genesis 1 is hurled like a lightning bolt from so many "gods" of this world that we need a true doctrinal examination of its credibility.

What does it mean to be made in the image of God? First of all, will all who use this verse to justify man's innate goodness yield on the doctrine of the special creation of man by a divine act of God? Will they, who want to flaunt this verse for their own uses, recognize the distinctly spiritual nature of man that differentiates him from all other creatures and makes him a morally responsible agent who must obey the commands of God like those He gave to Adam and Eve in the Garden of Eden? Will they recognize that God both did and still does give specific commands of behavior that He expects to be obeyed and that have consequences of disobedience? Or, are the purveyors of this verse only using this verse as Satan used half-truths to deceive Eve without any personal belief in the credibility of God to both institute commands and expect obedience to them? It is one thing for people to quote a verse and another thing for them to believe all the other doctrines related to the verses they want to quote and the biblical truths that spring from those passages.

What does it mean then that man was created in the image of God? It means that man is a reasoning being. It means that He has a mind that is forward thinking, planning, creating, pursuing goals, and planning strategies that are not immediate only. It also means that man is a spiritual being, not just a mass of neuro-driven chemicals that exists for today and is gone tomorrow. It means that man has a purpose both temporal and eternal. All these things are true both in Eden and beyond.

But there is more to being created in the image of God. Adam bore a likeness to God in that he was created without sin. God is holy and without sin. God also cannot sin. In this regard Adam was only created in the image of God and not God. Adam could sin as is seen in the fact that God gave him a specific command and specific punishment connected with that command. Man could choose to obey or not to obey. God, however, by the very nature of His holiness cannot sin, but man, a reflective image, could. And man did!

Charles Wesley wrote many songs to help the early Methodists learn doctrine and hold up under the assaults of an unfriendly social, governmental and ecclesiastical environment. His great Christmas carol "Hark! The Herald Angels Sing" is an example. Many Christians would know one verse without the hymnbook, but very few know all the stanzas. That is sad, because doctrine is important. Wesley wrote it because doctrine is important. Luther wrote hymns because doctrine is important. Many of our old hymns are written because the authors wanted to instill in the singers the very essential truths of Christian doctrine. We need to sing more old hymns today and learn more verses.

One verse that is often left out of many modern hymnals in "Hark! The Herald Angels Sing" goes like this: *"Come Desire of nations come! Fix in us Thy humble home. Rise the woman's conquering Seed, bruise in us the serpent's head. Adam's likeness now efface, stamp Thine image in its place; Second Adam from above, reinstate us in Thy love.*" Wow! There is a whole lot of doctrine of Christ and the apostles in that stanza.

This stanza helps to explain the answer to the question, "Are we not created in God's image?" Yes and no is the simple answer. We are still reasoning and eternal beings. But, we no longer possess the quality of being without sin. If those who believe we still retain the full image of God were to read a few more pages of the Bible from Genesis 1 to Genesis 5 they would find this very clear doctrine of scripture. *"And Adam lived one hundred and thirty years and* **begat a son in his own likeness, after his image**, *and named him Seth."* (Genesis 5:3) While we bear a partial image of God, we bear also the very corrupt nature of Adam and his sin.

The argument goes, "can a homosexual be wrong since he is made in the image of God?" The eternal reasoning being is in the image of God. The sinful behavior is in the image of Adam. Charles Wesley clearly captured this doctrine when he said, "Adam's likeness now efface; stamp Thine image in its place." The whole doctrine of the sinful nature of man is presented here. The image of God was corrupted, defaced and horribly marred by Adam's sin. He passed that along to all succeeding generations. All succeeding generations are now begotten in the image of Adam and in his likeness. The image of God must be recreated in man through the new birth. The image of Christ must be stamped in the place of man's image. To have that done requires a new birth as Jesus demands in John 3:3-6 and to be made a new creation as Paul describe in II Corinthians 5:17, *"Therefore if any man be in Christ, he is a new creature: old things are passed away; behold, all things are become new."*

Our current image is the image of sin and death. God describes that image in Romans 3:10-12, *"As it is written: 'There is none righteous, no, not one; there is none who understands, there is none who seeks after God. They have all turned aside; they have altogether become unprofitable; there is none who does good, no, not one.'"* Paul put it later in Romans 3:23, *"All have sinned and come short of the glory of*

God." The image of full godlikeness is simply not to be found in natural man.

God created man without sin and became man's adversary when man did sin. God gave clear commands as to the behavior that He expected and when it wasn't done He didn't say, "Well, that's all right. You are made after my image so you can't really have done anything wrong." No, that is not what God said. What God did say was, *"Of every tree of the garden you may freely eat, but of the tree of the knowledge of good and evil you shall not eat, for in the day that you eat of it you shall surely die."* (Genesis 2:16-17) He didn't say He would overlook sin because we were made in His image. He said that the wages of sin is death. He didn't say that man could use the excuse that He was made in the image of God to act and do as he willed. He said that His rules were to be obeyed. He didn't say that being made in His image made everything we want to do or be correct. He did say, *"Be ye holy, for I the Lord your God am holy."* (Leviticus 19:2)

When Adam disobeyed God he broke fellowship with His creator and friend. Now he had to live in fear, first of God's anger, then of death, then of the curse on the ground and then of his fellow man. He tried to hide his first fear with fig leaves, but God rejected that as an antidote to his disobedience. But God was gracious. He gave Adam and Eve the promise of a Savior who would come through the seed of the woman. He, the *"woman's conquering Seed",* would bring a defeat of sin and death and a reconciliation between God and men. This *"offspring of the Virgin's womb"* would make it possible for Adam's likeness to be effaced and for God's image to be stamped again in its place. The conditions that God placed were repent, turn from your sins, and embrace the Virgin's Son.

Repentance does not demand that God accept us as we are because we are created in His image. Repentance demands that we realize who we are, sinners by birth and nature from Adam, and then turning from that sin to Christ. The book of First John says, *"If we say we have no sin the truth is not in us."* (I John 1:8)

Many want to say that our natural man is made in the likeness of God. That is a false doctrine that leads only to destruction.

CHAPTER EIGHT

AS GOOD AS IT GETS?

The true nature of man leads us to the next argument that Mr. Thomas makes[1]. It is found in Genesis 1:31. *"Then God saw everything that He had made, and indeed it was very good. So the evening and the morning were the sixth day."* Mr. Thomas wants us to believe that he believes this verse and he makes that assumption clearly understood by using it as the basis of his argument. Again we have to ask whether the verse is a smokescreen of logic for him or a matter of faith. The whole verse says that this happened on the sixth day. If Mr. Thomas doesn't believe it was really the sixth day and but rather the sixth eon of billions of years then he has no genuine belief that this verse is really relevant to anything. The Bible is a whole, not a disjointed composite of unrelated parts.

God saw that everything was good on the sixth day. That is important. Timing, as the saying goes, is everything. A person can have a beautiful sleek car with shiny chrome and fancy hubcaps, but if the timing is off it isn't going to go anywhere. A comedian can have a really funny joke, but if the timing is off it won't get any laughs. A trapeze artist may have the greatest daring to fly through the air and soar from one trapeze to another, but if his timing is off he will face a disastrous fall. Timing is everything. For Mr. Thomas's argument this is very important.

Throughout Genesis chapter one God sees His work and it is noted that it was good. (Verses 10, 12, 18, 21, 25) This culminates with the summation that it was *"very good"* in verse 31. All this happened in the first six days of creation. It happened when the world was in a state of perfection and man was still living in the "image of God". But this was not the last word of God concerning the nature and condition of creation. We must always read on. We cannot let Mr. Thomas continue to shorten the field.

In Genesis chapter 3, two chapters past where Mr. Thomas wants to stop his critical analysis of God's view of creation, we have the great disaster of mankind. Eve, prompted by Satan's questioning of God's integrity (just like Mr. Thomas's questioning of God's integrity) ate the forbidden fruit. Adam then was prompted by Eve and he ate the forbidden fruit. The "all was good" part ended there. The train stopped at this station and the peace, harmony and perfection of creation are marred until the full coming of the "woman's conquering seed" will restore all things.

Let us begin in Genesis 3:14. *"So the Lord said to the serpent;* *'because you have done this* **you are CURSED'***…"* God continued his comments now to Eve in verse 16, *"To the woman he said, 'I will greatly* **multiply your sorrow** *in conception* **and in pain** *shall you bring forth children'…"* God is not done. To Adam He said in verses 17-19, *"***Cursed is the ground for your sake;*** in toil you shall eat of it all the days of your life.* **Both thorns and thistles it shall bring forth** *for you, and you shall eat the herb of the field.* **In the sweat of your face** *you shall eat bread* **till you return to the ground** *(die)"*.

Curses, pain, sorrow and hard toil are not the picture of perfection or a right summation of "it was very good". God said to Adam that all this happened *"for your sake"*. Adam had sinned. He had deliberately defied his Friend and his Maker. He had broken God's clearly set rules and that had a very real consequence. Eden's peace was gone. At the end of Genesis chapter three God drove Adam and Eve from the Garden of Eden. All was not good anymore. Adam and Eve had spiritually died as a consequence of their sin. Then God told them that they would return to the ground, physically die, as a consequence of their sin. The very ground they walked on had now been corrupted, cursed, because of their sin. There would be sorrow now in their peaceful little family and there would be fear and enmity with God. Mr. Thomas's thoughts that "all was very good" seem to lack any credibility at all.

But if we back up to chapter two of Genesis, before this awful act of sin against a righteous, loving and good God, we will find something that maybe Mr. Thomas will not like quite so much. What was the condition of man's relationship with man prior to the day of sin and punishment? Well, it was this. There was a man and there was a woman. Note this very clearly. When "it was good" there was a man and there was a woman. That was how God made it when it was good. That was how God planned it to be good, not just then but always.

Timing is everything. When it was good there was man and woman. After the fall of man into sin and the reproduction of man after his image we will find all manner of wickedness in this world. In Genesis 6:5 God comments on the nature of man; *"Then the Lord saw that the wickedness of man was great in the earth, and that every intent and thoughts of his heart were only evil continually."* Does this sound good? No! After the Great Flood God adds a further comment to Noah about the nature of man in Genesis 8:21, *"the imagination of man's heart is evil from his youth..."* The word for youth here is from a very young age. Toddlerhood might be a good translation. Does this sound good? No!

Timing is everything. Where do we find the account of Sodom and Gomorrah? Do we find it during the period of Genesis chapters 1 and 2, during the season of "it was very good" and before the curse of God on Adam's sin and the reproduction of mankind after the sinful nature of Adam? No. Actually we find it in Genesis chapters 18 and 19. Sadly this is even after mankind had recovered from the Great Flood. Although mankind had seen the power of the judgment of God, the very core of man's being, his flesh, his sin nature, would ignore the warnings and open judgment of God and go on pursuing their natural course of fleshly desire. The sin nature left to itself would be content to *"enjoy the pleasures of sin for a season"* (Hebrews 11:25) without regard to the temporal or eternal consequences of the same. This was clearly evident at the time of Sodom and Gomorrah and it is clearly evident today.

The sin nature of man that passed from Adam to all his generations did not drown in the flood. The sin nature was in the genetic makeup of the eight passengers aboard the ark. The sin nature came off the ark and reproduced on to the succeeding generations of the sons of Adam down to this day. As the sin nature has horribly marred the "image of God" in which Adam was created, it also has caused the marring of all creation from the ideal image of "it was very good". The reality is that we live in a cursed world inhabited by cursed humanity in need of a champion to break the power of the curse.

God has given us that Champion. God promised that Champion when the curse was given. To Satan he said, *"I will put enmity between you and the woman, and between your seed and her Seed; He shall bruise your head, and you shall bruise His heel."* (Genesis 3:15) Jesus Christ, the Seed of woman (notice here the first promise of the virgin birth), would triumph over Satan. He has the power to restore fallen humanity one person at a time to the will and way of God the Father Almighty. Each person who embraces Jesus Christ by faith is reborn of God's Spirit and recreated in Christ. Now that individual can live by the power of the Holy Spirit to demonstrate the holy life of Christ to the glory of God the Father by putting off the deeds of the flesh, including homosexual behavior, and live in the blessed hope of the return of Jesus Christ who will restore all things.

Adam's sin brought a number of curses. Sorrow, pain and death were three of them. Revelation 21:4 makes a glorious promise of the age to come when Christ has returned. *"And God will wipe away every tear from their eyes; there shall be no more death, nor sorrow, nor crying. There shall be no more pain, for the former things have passed away."* As Christ will change the nature of creation when He returns, He will change the nature of our sinful man into His glorious likeness even while we await his coming. This is why Paul can say, *"If any man be in Christ he is a new creation. Old things have passed away. Behold all things have become new."* (II Corinthians 5:17) Paul talked about some of the things that will change in I Corinthians 6:9-11. *"Do you not know that the unrighteous will not inherit the kingdom of God? Do not be deceived. Neither fornicators, not idolaters, not adulterers, nor homosexuals, nor sodomites, not thieves, nor covetous, nor drunkards, nor revilers, nor extortioners will inherit the kingdom of God.* **_And such were some of you._** *But you were washed, but you were sanctified, but you were justified in the name of the Lord Jesus and by the Spirit of our God."*

Acts chapter two records the first sermon Peter preached in Jerusalem after the crucifixion, resurrection and ascension of our Lord Jesus Christ. When he pointed out the sins of the people it records for us in verse 37, *"Now when they heard this, they were cut to the heart and said...what shall we do?"* Peter answered, *"Repent and be baptized in the Name of Jesus Christ."* Two things were necessary to take place. First the people had to recognize they were sinners and then they had to repent. Whenever anyone says that they are OK as they are, there can be no repentance because there has been no admission of sin.

After the judgment of the Great Flood people returned to the same old practices of sin and wickedness as they had lived in before. In the book of Revelation when God is pouring out His judgments on the earth it says that many will not repent. Instead it says that *"They blasphemed the God of heaven because of their pains and their sores, and did not repent of their deeds."* (Revelation 16:11)

Times haven't changed much. But timing is everything. *"It is appointed on to man once to die and after that the judgment."* (Hebrews 9:27) We have this time only to repent and prepare for eternity. If our timing is off, our condemnation is sure.

CHAPTER NINE

BUT IS IT RELEVANT?

The essential question that Mr. Thomas keeps trying to ask is simply if the Bible is really relevant. He does this through misrepresentation of the truth. He does this through using half quotes of biblical passages that gut the meaning of the whole text. He does this repeatedly in his article by mocking the perfect law that God gave to Israel in the Old Testament. "Is it relevant" is really the question that he asks over and over again.

The first question we could ask in response is, "Why is there law?" There are all kinds of laws on the books in cities around the United States that would beg the question, "Why is that a law?" Why is there a speed limit? Why is there an age for mandatory education? Why are there laws about what can be hunted and when it can be hunted? Lawyers contest the validity of laws all the time. Mr. Thomas is a lawyer. He is used to contending the validity of man's laws, sometimes quite rightfully so, but now he is contending the validity of God's law.

Mr. Thomas is not alone in this desire. Satan wants to contest God's law as well. He used the techniques of Mr. Thomas in his deception of Eve. So, maybe it is first of all important to know that we don't have to know all the reasons for God's laws. Paul wrote to the Romans concerning the judgments of God, *"How unsearchable are His judgments and His ways past finding out."* (Romans 11:33) Moses gave a companion verse to this in Deuteronomy 29:29. *"The secret things belong to the Lord our God, but those things which are revealed belong to us and to our children forever, that we may do all the words of this law."*

That is not to say that God does not reveal some of the reasons for His laws in His holy word. In Leviticus, the book that Mr. Thomas most loves to mock, God gives a reason for giving Israel laws to live by. In chapter 18, the very heart of Mr. Thomas's ire, God said, *"I am the Lord your God. According to the doings of the land of Egypt, where you dwelt, you shall not do; and according to the doings of the land of Canaan, where I am bringing you, you shall not do; nor shall you walk in their ordinances. You shall observe My judgments and keep My ordinances, to walk in them: I am the Lord your God."* (Vs. 2-4) That introduced the reasoning. He said, "I am the Lord and I am giving you the land." What could be clearer? I made you, I am providing for you, you live under my roof, obey my laws. But God goes on to make further explanation. After he lists a set of does and don'ts He said of the don'ts, *"For all these abominations the men of the land have done, who were before you, and thus the land is defiled."* (Vs. 27) He went on to say that if Israel did those abominations that the land would vomit them out and that they would be cut off as His chosen people. A parent might say this to a child. This is my house and these are my rules. God has a greater right to this statement.

Why these particular ones were the ones that God chose He doesn't have to explain. He is, after all, God. Sexual immorality, which is a big issue in Leviticus 18, is something that God has clearly stated throughout the Bible from Genesis to Leviticus that He doesn't like. He wants His people to be like Him. So he makes that clear in Leviticus 19:2, *"You shall be holy, for I the Lord your God am holy."* God's desire is for His people to reflect His nature. God did give the Israelites the clear option to do what He hated. He just told them there would be consequences for the behavior. The consequence was that they would be cut off from being His people.

That is the crux of the matter when people want to say that it is OK in God's church to live in the abominations that God has rejected. "It is not OK," God says, "and you cannot be called My people if you do it." That is God's statement, not that of mere man. You cannot handle the sacraments or ordinances of My church, My true people, if you practice the wickedness of Canaan. "My people," God says, "will call Me holy and follow my rules of holiness."

The Canaanites lived lives of absolute sexual debauchery and God said that it was a curse on the land. That is exactly what God said to Adam. For your sake the land is cursed. God is consistent. He cursed the land for Adam's sin and He cursed the land for the Canaanites' sin and He would curse the land again if Israel tried to imitate the Canaanites instead of God. The entire Bible ties together. Canaan was described as a land flowing with milk and honey. It was a wonderful place and the wicked inhabitants were being kicked out of it. Does that sound familiar? That is exactly what God did to Adam and Eve when they sinned against Him. He kicked them out of the wonderful place they lived.

God will still do the same today. He will remove His blessings from the church which has polluted itself with the wickedness of Canaan. While it may keep a church name on the door, God will have said, "You are not My church."

God doesn't need to explain His rules. What He has told us is that He has loved His people, that He has saved them from the misery of slavery to sin, that He is watching over them and providing all the things they might need and that He expects them to listen and obey the rules He gives them. He doesn't want excuses. He doesn't want argument. He wants obedience. He said it clearly to the excuse making King Saul, *"To obey is better than sacrifice and to heed than the fat of rams."* (I Samuel 15:22)

But the real problem for all those who argue with God is not a lack of understanding. It is the spirit of rebellion in man that insists on doing things our own way. But it goes beyond that. It is the need for self-justification and to either get verification of our innate rightness from an authority or to discredit that authority so that we can still appear right. Unfortunately for those who try to practice this charade with God, He is not going to go away and He is not going to change His mind. It is up to man to fall on His face and say, "Be merciful to me a sinner."

And that brings us to the real point of the law and its relevance. The law was given so that we could see how far short of God we are and throw ourselves on Him for our salvation. The law was to lead us to Christ. Paul made a lengthy statement about this purpose of the law in Galatians 3:19-24. ***"What purpose then does the law serve?*** *It was added because of transgressions, till the Seed should come to whom the promise was made; and it was appointed through angels by the hand of a mediator. Now a mediator does not mediate for one only, but God is one. Is the law then against the promises of God? Certainly not! For if there had been a law given which could have given life, truly righteousness would have been by the law. But the Scripture has confined all under sin that the promise by faith in Jesus Christ might be given to those who believe. But before faith came, we were kept under guard by the law, kept for the faith which would afterward be revealed.* **Therefore the law was our tutor to bring us to Christ,** *that we might be justified by faith."*

The law was given by a loving God to steer us away from sin that would bring on us the severe judgment of God and to direct us to a course of freedom from the curse of our own failed nature. The law is good, but we can't keep it. We can't keep it because it is contrary to our nature of sin passed on to us by our first sire Adam. The law brings judgment to those who break it. The Bible clearly and repeatedly says that we all break it. When Solomon dedicated his temple and made that wonderful prayer of dedication, he said in I Kings 8:46, *"When they sin against You (for there is no one who does not sin)..."* Paul echoed this in Romans 3:23, *"For all have sinned and come short of the glory of God."* It is the clearest possible teaching of the entire

Bible, we all sin. Because we all sin we need a remedy for sin. The law teaches us that lesson and then it clearly points to the One, the seed of woman, the promised Savior, the only hope from our miserable condition and judgment of sin, it points to Jesus.

Or not! What? The other choice is that it points to our rejection of the law as a relevant and true statement of God. If what we are doing is what we want to do and we have no fear of God before our eyes and thus no shame in doing what we want to do, then there is recourse other than falling on Jesus for our salvation. It is to say that we don't have any sin. It is to say that the law is irrelevant. We can try to say that some whacky old dude overheated by the desert air had some kind of stomach upset and in the midst of that made a lot of laws that no one then or now has any real need of obeying.

Mr. Thomas says that the mainstream church has moved beyond the primitive rituals of Levitical practice. Christianity moved beyond animal sacrifice because Christ was sacrificed once for all as the writer of Hebrews in the New Testament makes clear. As a trained minister Mr. Thomas knows that but selectively seeks to avoid that truth to make his point that Leviticus is irrelevant. But no scripture is irrelevant. *"All Scripture is inspired by God and profitable . . ."* and that includes Leviticus and the entire Old Testament.

What are irrelevant are the opinions of "mainstream" religion if they disagree with the opinions of God. The purpose of the church is to speak forth the Word of God and not make up our own to satisfy our own wants and desires. When "mainstream" religion does this it becomes irrelevant. It will not be the Word of God that stops having meaning. It will remain the basis both for life and for judgment. The opinions of man will change again in a few years, but the Word of God will endure. If "mainstream" religion has "grown beyond" the Word of God then it has no more practical use for a world in need. The Law teaches us our failure and leads us to our solution – Jesus

Christ. Any other message is not a biblical one and is irrelevant to the needs of mankind.

CHAPTER TEN

CANAAN'S NOT SO FAIR AND PLEASANT LAND

Since Mr. Thomas has been so hostile to Leviticus 18 maybe we should stop a moment and consider what the chapter does say. Is it really the bogeyman of the Bible that he makes it out to be? Has he been honest with the sum of its contents or just picky for a purpose? Would he propose that we ignore all of Leviticus 18 or just the part that offends him?

Remember that God had proscribed to His people Israel all the heathen practices of Canaan. In Leviticus 18:3 He said, *"And according to the doings of the land of Canaan, where I am bringing you, you shall not do; nor shall you walk in their ordinances."* He gave the result of the evil practices of Canaan in Leviticus 18:24-25. *"Do not defile yourselves with any of these things; for by all these the nations are defiled, which I am casting out before you. For the land is defiled; therefore I visit the punishment of its iniquity upon it, and the land vomits out its inhabitants."* Between verse three and verse twenty-four we have a list of proscriptions; all but one of them clearly sexual in content, that God gave to His holy people.

Here begins the absurdity of Mr. Thomas's arguments. Seven items are banned. Six of them are purely sexual. Mr. Thomas takes umbrage with one. Does that mean that 86% of the laws of God are good and right? According to Mr. Thomas's article that would be an absurd conclusion to make. He has mocked the law of God, but in chapter 18 he mocks only one of seven laws. Why? I can't answer that for Mr. Thomas, but it raises the question about how he feels about the other six laws.

So, what are these seven banned practices? First there is incest. Verses six through sixteen, eleven verses, deal with all the relationships of family that would be incestuous. Apparently Mr. Thomas is OK with God saying that incest is wrong. Those who want to practice it might disagree with Mr. Thomas and seek to delete this practice as sin. After all, what is good for one immoral practice should be good for another!

Next on the list is familial cohabitation. This is the practice of taking a woman and her sister or a woman and her mother or a woman and her daughter to be co-spouses. Since bigamy is illegal in America, Mr. Thomas dare not promote this practice. The third item on the list is the practice of sexual intercourse while a woman is having her menstrual period. Again, Mr. Thomas does not object. Maybe he does, but he doesn't take the time to do it in his article. Fourth on the list is adultery. Well, God did ban adultery in the Ten Commandments so it would be pretty brazen of Mr. Thomas to promote it as a side issue of Scripture.

The next item on the list is not really sexual in nature, but it has its roots in the Canaanite sexual practices. Infanticide is item number five. This evil practice was done at the altar to Molech (Moloch). According to rabbinical writing we have this description of the practice:

"Tophet is Moloch, which was made of brass; and they heated him from his lower parts; and his hands being stretched out, and made hot, they put the child between his hands, and it was burnt; when it vehemently cried out; but the priests beat a drum, that the father might not hear the voice of his son, and his heart might not be moved." The 12th-century Rashi, commenting on Jeremiah 7:31[1].

Far more graphic descriptions are available from more

contemporary Greek and Roman sources, but it is enough to be said that God prohibited this practice. I wonder how Mr. Thomas feels about abortion. For the Canaanite, infanticide done after birth was completely acceptable. They would have applauded the United States Supreme Court's decision to allow pre-natal murder of children. Sadly many people naming the name of Christ are indifferent or even supportive of this heathen practice of butchering the unborn. However Mr. Thomas may feel about abortion he doesn't condemn God's ban on burning babies and that is critical to the flaw in his argument.

Sixth on the list of banned practices is found in Leviticus 18:22, *"You shall not lie with a male as with a woman. It is an abomination."* After a list of five heathen practices that Mr. Thomas does not raise objections to God banning, we come to one that really raises his hackles. Can God be right five out of six times and completely blow it on number six? That would be an odd assumption, but Mr. Thomas clearly leaves us to believe that to be the case.

But we are not done with the list of heathen perversions that God banned. Last on the list is found in Leviticus 18:23, *"Nor shall you mate with an animal, to defile yourself with it. Nor shall any woman stand before an animal to mate with it. It is a perversion."* The term for this perversion is bestiality. It was a practice in the land of Canaan and God said that His holy people were not to follow any of the customs or ordinances of the Canaanite people. Certainly the ASPCA would applaud this edict of God. Apparently by his silence on the subject Mr. Thomas also concurs with God on this point.

Only on the abomination of sodomy does Mr. Thomas equivocate that God could have been in error. Maybe Mr. Thomas takes a Canaanite view of God as expressed in I Kings 18:27, *"Cry aloud, for he is a god; either he is meditating, or he is busy, or he is on a journey, or perhaps he is sleeping and must be awakened."* To the Canaanites the gods were very much like man in nature and conduct, although in many respects they were far more immoral. But, being humanlike they could take a break from their affairs of state to look after other interests. Perhaps this is Mr. Thomas's view of God, so while God was busy with other things Moses just inserted his own ideas and got this one on sodomy all wrong.

Maybe if it were only mentioned here Mr. Thomas could try to make his point, but it isn't just mentioned here. We have already seen in Genesis 19 how God destroyed Sodom and Gomorrah for their abominable practice. Is it elsewhere in the Old Testament record as well? God's condemnation of sodomy continues in Leviticus 20:13 where He imposes the death penalty on the practice just has He had imposed it Himself against Sodom. Again in Deuteronomy 23:18 God speaks of this practice, *"You shall not bring the wages of a harlot or the price of a dog to the house of the Lord your God for any vowed offering, for both of these are an abomination to the Lord your God."* The "price of a dog" is not the payment on a good golden retriever puppy. It is the wages of a male prostitute (qadesh) which were commonly found in Canaanite temples right next to the female prostitutes who also plied their trade there.

Sadly the people of God disobeyed Him and did not rid the land of Canaan of either the Canaanites or their religious practices. In Judges 19 the issue arose again. The tribe of Benjamin, one of the twelve tribes of Israel, had allowed open homosexuality to be practiced in their tribal territory. When there was an attempted rape of a visiting Levite, the consequence was a civil war in Israel that killed fifty thousand men and nearly obliterated the tribe of Benjamin. Even after that it is recorded in I Kings chapters 14, 15 and 22 as well as II Kings 23 that the evil practice of Canaanite religion was still existent in Israel.

The result of this sin was that God ultimately removed Israel from the land as He had intended for them to remove the Canaanites. In II Kings 17:7-23 God summed up his charges against the people. *"For so it was that the children of Israel had sinned against the Lord their God . . . and had walked in the statutes of the nations whom the Lord had cast out from before the children of Israel . . . (and) secretly did against the Lord their God things that were not right."* Like Adam had spoiled Eden and was evicted and as the Canaanites had spoiled Canaan and were to be evicted, God evicted His own people from the land for shamelessly doing the same deeds that were proscribed to them.

How deeply these practices were ingrained in Canaanite culture can be seen in Canaanite religious practices. Much about these practices can be gleaned from Scripture, but archaeology has added further and much more graphically horrible detail. In diggings at Ugarit (Syria) in the years between WWI and WWII, detailed writings were found and ultimately translated. They reveal a society so perverse that even the debauched of today might blanch at their deeds.

Their chief god, El, was remote, but his doings were well publicized. He had married three wives. They were his sisters[2]. Thus incest was common in Canaanite religion. Since they were sisters it was also not uncommon to have familial cohabitation. These were the first two practices that God banned to Israel in Leviticus 18. El could also step out of his remoteness into the realm of humanity to seduce fair maidens of his choice.

Subordinate to El was Baal. Baal's sister and wife was Anath. "Anath is represented often as a naked woman bestride a lion with a lily in one hand and a serpent in the other. The lily represented sex appeal and the serpent represented fertility.[3]" The word used for the male prostitutes who worked for the goddess Anath was qadesh (the dog in Deuteronomy 23).

Baal, along with the female deities Astarte and Asherah, were largely seen as fertility deities. Asherah was the supposed wife of El but was also the consort of Baal. (Adultery was simply a practice of being like the gods and was banned by God.) The basis of fertility cults was the idea that the more fertility rites were practiced in the temples of these gods and goddesses, the more likely people were to be successful in the practice of fertility in their homes and farms. The religious rites in these temples were nothing less than open sexual orgies involving men with men as well as men with women and even animals. "An Ugaritic myth tells of Anat (Anath), Baal's sister, trying to find Baal, god of water in all its forms. He has died (there is a drought), but Anat eventually finds him. When he sees her he is overcome with love. He has intercourse with her in the form of a cow.[4]" Here we can see God's law against bestiality.

In every detail we see the deeds of Canaan banned by God to His people who were to be holy. The stench of Canaanite sin reached heaven and they were expelled. God expects holiness in His church and we should not become like Israel, which became like Canaan. We cannot condone that which God has clearly condemned. We cannot accept Mr. Thomas's argument that God was wrong.

CHAPTER ELEVEN

NOT A MATTER OF CONJECTURE

Having ignored the bulk of Old Testament teaching about homosexuality, and after distorting that part that he did use, Mr. Thomas now moves to the New Testament where he practices the same sleight of hand. First, he does not quote a specific passage as he had in Leviticus, but makes a blanket assumption concerning all the New Testament teaching about homosexual behavior. This would leave his readers with the faulty assumption that the New Testament did not have anything specific to state on the subject. That would leave the door open for him to make his baseless assertion about what Paul might have meant when he addressed the issue of homosexuality being a sin. That would be wrong.

In Romans, I Corinthians and I Timothy we find three passages that specifically deal with homosexuality. First let us consider the three passages. Romans 1:26-29:

"For this reason God gave them up to vile passions. For even their women exchanged the natural use for what is against nature. Likewise also the men, leaving the natural use of the woman, burned in their lust for one another, men with men committing what is shameful, and receiving in themselves the penalty of their error which was due. And even as they did not like to retain God in their knowledge, God gave them over to a debased mind, to do those things which are not fitting; being filled with all

unrighteousness, sexual immorality, wickedness, covetousness, maliciousness; full of envy, murder, strife, deceit, evil-mindedness; they are whisperers."

1 Corinthians 6:9-10:

"Do you not know that the unrighteous will not inherit the kingdom of God? Do not be deceived. Neither fornicators, nor idolaters, nor adulterers, nor homosexuals, nor sodomites, nor thieves, nor covetous, nor drunkards, nor revilers, nor extortioners will inherit the kingdom of God."

1 Tim 1:9-10:

"Knowing this: that the law is not made for a righteous person, but for the lawless and insubordinate, for the ungodly and for sinners, for the unholy and profane, for murderers of fathers and murderers of mothers, for manslayers, for fornicators, for sodomites, for kidnappers, for liars, for perjurers, and if there is any other thing that is contrary to sound doctrine."

The New Testament is rife with passages about sexual immorality in general. These three passages include other types of sexual immorality along with homosexuality. It is logical then to see homosexuality included in the passages that speak of sexual immorality in a general sense and not listing all the specific kinds as found in these specific passages. Paul, for example, includes his list of the deeds of the flesh in Galatians 5:21 with the simple phrase, *"and the like"*. Not every list of sins is a complete list, but it is clear from the many lists that homosexual behavior is part of the greater heading of sexual immorality.

This would be the idea that Mr. Thomas is challenging. His assertion is that Paul is not talking about the general practice of homosexuality but about a specific practice of men keeping boys as sexual slaves. The term would be *pederasty*[1]. Since such a practice would be illegal in such a society as ours that outlaws sexual exploitation of minors, then the condemnation in Scripture of homosexual behavior is nothing we have to concern ourselves with in modern America. Since Paul is talking about an ancient, and now outlawed practice, we can scratch that deed of sexual immorality off the list.

When I was in high school we had to read *The Scarlet Letter*.

In Colonial America fornication was considered a sin because the Bible said it was. Hester got stuck with the scarlet letter "A" on her blouse. It was to let all know that she was sexually immoral. Today nearly 41% of all births in the United States are to single mothers[2]. Does this mean that fornication is no longer a sin because no one wears a scarlet letter anymore and out of wedlock births is so common? Since fornication is no longer a sin in our society, does that mean it is no longer a sin before God? That would be Mr. Thomas's logic, but it is not the whole case.

Mr. Thomas assumes that God is talking about pederasty. He uses the exact term "most likely" when stating what he concludes is God's opinion[3]. But what God is speaking of is not a matter of conjecture. God speaks very clearly and He uses words that have meaning. Conjecture is not necessary. If I say, "I want a piece of chocolate cake" it cannot be assumed that I "most likely" mean a piece of the yellow cake next to the chocolate cake in the display case. I would send the waitress back with the yellow cake because her assumption would be wrong. I said "chocolate cake" and that isn't open to interpretation. Neither is what God said.

The Greek language used in the New Testament, Koine Greek, is a very clear language. It was designed to make speech clearly understood by all the citizens of the vast Greek Empire founded by Alexander the Great. That world was inherited by the Romans who had the great sense to keep using the Greek language to unite their empire. This was the language in which the New Testament was written and into which the Old Testament was translated into the version called the Septuagint before the birth of Christ. The language is so clear that we know what is meant by what is said.

What is said by Paul in Romans chapter one leaves no possible honest interpretation that he meant pederasty. Paul's phrase "men with men" cannot be translated men with boys. Just like our language can differentiate between men and boys, so could the Greek. Paul could have used other words to express himself, but he didn't. He could have used the word *"paidion"* for boy or *"pais"* for young man, but he used *"arsenes"* for man. *"Men with men"* he states very clearly. If that were not enough he has already condemned the practice of lesbianism when he said *"For even their women exchanged the natural use for what is against nature."* The context of the two ideas together negates the possibility that Paul was referring to men taking young men into their homes for homosexual concubinage or sex slavery. Paul made absolutely no implication that women were using little girls or that men were using boys.

In the passages in Corinthians and Timothy, Paul used another term that likewise leaves no room for the misinterpretation by Mr. Thomas. In these verses he uses the term *"arsenokoitai"*. This word keeps the base root word for men *"arsenes"* as used in Romans chapter one. This word adds a second word to the first making it a compound word.

In English we use compound words all the time. Our grandchildren have all sat in the "highchair" at the table. It is a chair that is high. Compound words help us picture two things at one time. They clarify our language. Imagine having to think up an entirely different word for a chair that is high for a small child to sit in. That would be a long term to say a simple thing. In the Greek language it is the same way.

The term Paul used first stressed that men were involved. The second word that Paul used was one that is translated "coitus" in modern English. It is a simple compound word. A man with a man having sexual intercourse is the simplest and most straightforward translation. In Leviticus 18:22, *"You shall not lie with a male as with a woman. It is an abomination."* God called this practice an abomination. He gave an accurate description of the practice that does not include writing it off as some evil boy fetish of the ancient Romans. This was one of the key sins of the immoral Canaanites that God had forbidden to His people Israel. This is a sin that He denounces in the New Testament and says that those who practice it are not part of His kingdom. (I Corinthians 6:9-10) Whether it was a Canaanite, an Israelite, a Roman, a Greek or a modern American, God says it is still sin.

What must be clear is that God was not making exceptions in His law. Mr. Thomas upholds the modern concept that if God only understood that today men would only practice homosexuality in committed monogamous relationships, and that difference would make it right, then God would lift His prohibition against the practice. Does that mean that Mr. Thomas would call same sex practitioners who are not in monogamous committed relationships to be living in sin? Are all homosexuals living in sin who are still playing the field to find their one true mate? Or does Mr. Thomas just have an inadequate view of God and is playing with Him as a cat with a mouse?

Question leads to question but mostly it just demonstrates the desire to create a diminished God. This kind of God may suit the purposes of the homosexual agenda, but it does not picture the God of the Bible. It does not follow the teachings of the church that He is God the Father Almighty, maker of heaven and earth. It rejects the teaching of the church about all His other plans and works for men that have come from the gift of His Son Jesus Christ. While the homosexual agenda wants to create a different God, God is not surprised at their efforts.

God knew that men would keep practicing homosexual behaviors. He knew that they would try to justify their actions. He knew that they would reject His word and substitute their own ideas for His laws to call themselves good. He knew all this and in advance He said, "These are My rules; this is My church; this is My unchangeable verdict; you may choose your way, but I will choose your outcome."

Man can try to rewrite the Bible. Certainly Mr. Thomas has given his own attempt at it. It may persuade man, but it will not persuade God. The visible church may become as corrupt as a leprous garment but God is calling His true church to stand for His Word so that the world will have a witness to Him. The true church may not be able to stop corruption, but it can say that it will not stand with it or abide its practice in its midst. This is God's call of discipleship today.

CHAPTER TWELVE

THE BLAME GAME

Several years ago in a comic strip in our local paper a little girl asked her father, "Daddy, what is a half-truth?" His simple reply, "It is a whole lie." If we start with a premise that is half true and carry it to its logical conclusion, the conclusion will become a greater lie than the half true premise. Years ago my wife and I went to see the St. Louis Arch. It is very impressive. There was a video presentation about how it was made and I actually think that was more impressive. Every night after it got cool the engineers had to make calculations about the accuracy of the arch's angle of ascent. If that angle were off as much as a fraction of an inch at one hundred feet apart, then the two sides would not have met at the top. It was an absolute feat of engineering skill. That is what happens with a half true premise when carried to its logical conclusion. Its end is far distant from matching with truth.

Mr. Thomas began with a half-truth of human nature. He stopped in Genesis chapter one where God saw that His creation was good. He completely ignored that sin corrupted that creation and that the rest of the Scripture teaches that there is "none good, no not one." Using a faulty foundation of ignored truth, he wants to build on it that God is ultimately responsible for homosexual desire and practice. Since God instituted it in making man "good" then God cannot condemn those who practice it. The argument is, "It is God's fault (or design) that I am this way, so God must accept me as I am."

The corollary to this is the assertion, "I was born this way." The corollary is true. The premise that it is based upon is false. That's right. The corollary is true! As the old song says, "How do I know, the Bible tells me so!"

Unless we adopt the false doctrine of the Pelagians, that man is not born with original sin, we have to accept a Bible's worth of truth to the contrary. Solomon dedicated the temple with these words, *"When they sin against You (for there is no one who does not sin)"* (I Kings 8:46) and made it clear that all sin which is a direct contradiction to Pelagianism. David said in Psalm 51:5 *"Behold, I was brought forth in iniquity, and in sin my mother conceived me."* Since God commanded mankind to procreate, then conception is not a sin. David was describing the condition of his own soul at conception. Paul's clear argument in Romans 3 that *"there is none righteous, no not one"* and his final conclusion *"for all have sinned and come short of the glory of God"* state the real nature of mankind.

What does this mean? It means we are all born sinners. We are all born with a sin nature. We are all born with the desire to go our own way. Isaiah made it clear in chapter 53:6, *"All we like sheep have gone astray; we have turned, every one, to his own way; and the LORD has laid on Him the iniquity of us all."* From early childhood on we rebel against our parents, our teachers and other authorities. God said of us, *"the imagination of man's heart is evil from his youth."* (Gen. 8:21) The accuracy of Mr. Thomas's foundational argument that we are good is truly without foundation. Therefore the house he builds from it is foundationless.

But the corollary to his argument that we are born a certain way is true. We are all born sinners and wanting to sin. We want to do what we want to do. We are born in rebellion to God and only through the love of God demonstrated in the death of His own Son on the cross for our sins can we become good and right. Prior to falling at Christ's feet in repentant faith, we are all vile, or as Isaiah said in chapter 64:6, *"But we are all like an unclean thing, and all our righteousnesses are like filthy rags."* Prior to coming to Christ we are practitioners of every evil thing in our nature. Paul said in I Corinthians 6:9-11, *"Do you not know that the unrighteous will not inherit the kingdom of God? Do not be deceived. Neither fornicators, nor idolaters, nor adulterers, nor homosexuals, nor sodomites, nor thieves, nor covetous, nor drunkards, nor revilers, nor extortioners will inherit the kingdom of God.* **And such were some of you.** *But you were washed, but you were sanctified, but you were justified in the name of the Lord Jesus and by the Spirit of our God."*

Notice particularly Paul's comment *"and such were some of you."* There is a nasty list of sins that Paul has given. Then he says, *"and such **were** some of you."* Before they were born again into the kingdom of God they were one way. After they were born again into the kingdom of God they were not that way anymore. Their sins were washed away in Christ and they became a new creation. The old was passed and they became new. They were born again. The Holy Spirit has now exploded into their lives with power to overcome the sins that had beset them prior to their salvation. When they were born, they were born to sin. When they were born again, they were born again to righteousness in Jesus Christ.

Every child who is born into this world is born to sin. Every child has it within himself or herself to be a murderer, a drunkard, a thief, a liar, an adulterer, a cheat or a homosexual. It is part of the nature of our birth. The Bible says so. That is how we are born as Adam's children. We cannot dismiss the argument that the homosexual makes that he or she was born that way. We all were.

The problem is that both those within the church and those outside the church become too self-righteous about things we "haven't done". We would like to ignore the fact that we have really been doing "those bad things" since we were old enough to act out on them.

Let us consider carefully what Jesus has to say about our sinfulness. In Matthew 5:27-28 he said, *"You have heard that it was said to those of old, 'You shall not commit adultery.' But I say to you that whoever looks at a woman to lust for her has already committed adultery with her in his heart."* That is harsh. There are a lot of people who would "never" commit the act in the flesh but are just as guilty before God for having committed the act with a look and a thought. How about murder? Our jails would be full if the truth were fully known. Jesus said in Matthew 5:21-22, *"You have heard that it was said to those of old, 'You shall not murder, and whoever murders will be in danger of the judgment.' But I say to you that whoever is angry with his brother without a cause shall be in danger of the judgment. And whoever says to his brother, 'Raca!' shall be in danger of the council. But whoever says, 'You fool!' shall be in danger of hell fire."* Jesus made it clear that sin is a heart condition, not just a matter of acting things out. He further stated in Matthew 10:19-20, *"For out of the heart proceed evil thoughts, murders, adulteries, fornications, thefts, false witness, (and) blasphemies. These are the things which defile a man."*

All sinful behavior is the product of sinful heart. The hater or the murderer; the luster or the adulterer; the covetous or the thief; the philosophical humanist or the homosexual; it all begins in the heart of sin. Whether it ever moves to the deeds of the flesh in such extreme behaviors is not really the issue. God sees the heart of us all. What is there He sees. It is our nature to blame others for being a worse sinner than us so that we are justified. But justification can only come from God. That justification comes through the blood of His Son Jesus Christ.

It is also our nature, however, to blame others for our sinful condition. Let us look at man's first sin and consider the whole text of Genesis 3:9-13. *"Then the LORD God called to Adam and said to him, "Where are you?" So he said, "I heard Your voice in the garden, and I was afraid because I was naked; and I hid myself."* **And He (God) said**, *"Who told you that you were naked?* **Have you eaten from the tree** *of which I commanded you that you should not* *eat?"* **Then the man said, "The woman whom You gave to be with me, she gave me** *of the tree, and I ate."* **And the LORD God said to the woman, "What is this you have done?"** **The woman said, "The serpent deceived me,** *and I ate."*

Notice the blame game being played out here. Adam was not at fault, of course. None of us are. Adam has two people to blame. First he blamed God. "The woman YOU GAVE me," he said. Since you gave her to me, God, you can't blame me for doing what I did. Do you hear the argument of the homosexual community? Since you made me this way God, I can't be blamed for what I am doing. But Adam was not done. "The woman gave it to me," he added. It was just a response to my environment or familial condition. The homosexual argument is here as well. I got this from my mother or father's gene pool. Don't look at me. God did not, by the way, accept Adam's argument. God had given a command and He expected it to be obeyed. He will not accept the argument of any human as their behavior that violates His standard of holiness. He expects to be obeyed. He wants us to obey Him and not make excuses.

Now we see Eve following the pattern of her husband. "It's not my fault; the serpent tricked me." What she was saying is, "If I just had known right from wrong I wouldn't have been tricked, so God it is really your fault."

Blaming God for sin doesn't make God guilty. It didn't fly with God when Adam said it and it didn't fly with God when Eve said it. It won't fly with God when anyone says it. God is holy and sinless. We cannot make the same claim. God made us good and we sinned. Our nature now is to sin and want to sin. Our second nature is to blame anyone or anything else for our sin so that we don't have to bear any guilt for it. It is a common legal maneuver to blame someone else for the sin of the accused. Mr. Thomas is a lawyer. He may use this argument in the court of man and win, but he will never win this argument in the court of God.

CHAPTER THIRTEEN

GREATER EXPECTATIONS

A common confessional creed is found in I John 1:8-9. *"If we say that we have no sin, we deceive ourselves, and the truth is not in us. If we confess our sins, He is faithful and just to forgive us our sins and to cleanse us from all unrighteousness."* After this creed is spoken, a pause for reflection is taken in order for those making this profession to give silent thought and confession of their personal sins.

But what if they think they don't have any? This would be a great irony since they just confessed that they know not the truth if they think they have no sin. Verse ten of I John 1 makes the case against them even more egregious. They call God a liar. *"If we say that we have not sinned, we make Him a liar, and His word is not in us."* So, it is God then that sets the standard. When we understand this we can come with Paul to God and say, *"O wretched man that I am! Who will deliver me from this body of death?"* (Romans 7:24) And again we would say with Paul, *"For I know that in me (that is, in my flesh) nothing good dwells."* (Romans 7:18)

But what if we disagree with this? Then we disagree with God. God has made the indictment against our sinful practice and our sinful nature. It is up to us to let Him make the definition and consequent condemnation for sin and it is up to us to make true confession. This is where the rubber meets the road, so to speak. If we say that what we are doing is not sinful, when God says that it is, then the truth is not in us, His word is not in us and we are not His. God expects His children to leave Him in the position of authority. He expects to be held as all wise. He expects those who are truly His, the spiritual church, to respond differently to Him than the world at large. He sets for His true church greater expectations.

It is with this teaching clearly understood by the church that Paul said to the Corinthians in I Corinthians 6:11, *"And such were some of you. But you were washed, but you were sanctified, but you were justified in the name of the Lord Jesus and by the Spirit of our God."* The words, *"such were"*, clearly states a change had taken place. They had believed God to be true. They had believed that His definition of their behavior was the one that counted and that His just indictment against it was legitimate. Consequently, having seen the just judgment for their sins they had fallen upon the grace of God in Jesus Christ and now sought to live their lives by the power of the Holy Spirit. No longer did they wish to live as they were in the sins that God had condemned, but they wished to live for Him. This change of perception did not destroy the desires of the flesh to live in its natural condition of sin, but it gave the believer power in the Spirit to know that the desires were wrong and to live in the righteous fashion of Christ.

This call by God to live in the newness of life, being born again from sin and judgment to eternal life as God's children, is repeated throughout the New Testament. Indeed, one short chapter in this book would not be adequate to give them all in full detail. All of Romans chapters 6-8 are dedicated to this teaching. I Corinthians 6, Galatians 5, Ephesians 4 and 5, Colossians 3, and I Peter 4 are all teaching this doctrine. In fact, the weight of all the New Testament epistles is to make clear that based on a person's new life in Christ, there is to be a new way of life. Paul set it forth clearly and succinctly to the church at Thessalonica when he said, *"For they themselves (all the people in the surrounding region of Thessalonica) declare concerning us what manner of entry we had to you, and* **how you turned to God from idols to serve the living and true God."** (I Thessalonians 1:9)

They turned to God and from their former way of life. They didn't say to God that their former way of life was OK. They didn't try to justify their former way of life which was corrupted by the immorality of pagan idols. They didn't try to say that since God had made gold He must have meant it to be worshipped as an idol. They didn't say to God that since He made man with desires that it must be OK to fulfill them. No, they turned to God and that left them with their backs turned to the life of idolatry and immorality that idol worship entailed. The old ways brought only emptiness and death. God offered them forgiveness and life. They could not have both the old and the new, and so having turned to God they turned from their old life.

Putting off the old and putting on the new is a figure of speech that depicts death to the old life of sin and embracing the new life in Christ. Paul said to the Colossians, *"Therefore put to death your members which are on the earth: fornication, uncleanness, passion, evil desire, and covetousness, which is idolatry. Because of these things the wrath of God is coming upon the sons of disobedience, in which you yourselves once walked when you lived in them. But now you yourselves are to put off all these."* (Colossians 3:5-8) Then in verse ten of the same chapter Paul wrote, *"Put on the new man who is renewed in the knowledge of Him who created Him."* The new man will be alert to the teaching of God, *"the knowledge of Him",* and will walk in obedience to that knowledge. Their source for decision making will not be man's wisdom, but God's. Their directions will not come from self-desire but from the teachings of God's word. Those who heard Paul, those who had trusted Christ for their salvation, believed that if God could be trusted to tell the truth about their salvation He could also be trusted to tell the truth about their walk of holiness. His word was true across the board.

This same challenge to "put off" and "put on" was given to

the church at Ephesus. In Ephesians he put the challenge in the context of the renewed mind in Christ to the old mind full of vanity and futility in the world. In chapter 4:17-21 he teaches, *"This I say, therefore, and testify in the Lord, that you should no longer walk as the rest of the Gentiles walk, in the futility of their mind, having their understanding darkened, being alienated from the life of God, because of the ignorance that is in them, because of the blindness of their heart; who, being past feeling, have given themselves over to lewdness, to work all uncleanness with greediness. But you have not so learned Christ, if indeed you have heard Him and have been taught by Him, as the truth is in Jesus."* The old mind and the old man were full of lewdness and corruption, but Christ taught a different way. Therefore Paul said *"put off"* (Vs. 22), *"be renewed in the spirit of your mind"* (Vs. 23) and *"put on"* (Vs. 24). Once again we see the need to be taught a new way and we find that way in the word of God, the teachings of the truth of Christ.

The difficulty is that we like the old way. It is our natural condition and it is easy to do. We are sinners and we like to sin. Paul addressed this in Galatians 5 where he first lists the deeds of the flesh. They are not all the deeds of the flesh that could be listed so he concludes his list with the words *"and such like"*. The list is still quite comprehensive. In verse 19 he covered sexual sins. In verse 20 he covered spiritual sins. In verse 21 he covered other behavioral sins not already listed. This, he said, is our flesh. It is the natural yearning of the body, mind and spirit to do these things. Opposed to these things is the will of God as lived out in the fruit of the Spirit as listed in verses 22 and 23. These two natures, the old nature of the flesh and the new nature from being born again by the Spirit of God, are at warfare. Who we listen to, who we walk with, will determine who we are.

The Holy Spirit will teach us through the word of God. Paul told Timothy that the Bible is the God breathed word of God (perhaps literally – *the very breath or Spirit of God*) and *"is profitable for doctrine, reproof, correction and instruction in righteousness."* (II

Timothy 3:16) It is by this word that we will be *"transformed by the renewing of your mind that you may prove what is that good and acceptable and perfect will of God".* (Romans 12:2) And what does the Holy Spirit declare to us from God's Holy Word? It seems to come to us from Leviticus chapter 19, right after that vilified passage in the Old Testament that has so aroused the homosexual community against trusting the word of God to be true. It is the summation of all that God said in chapter 18 and it is quoted for us in I Peter 1:15 and 16 as the standard of practice for those who wish to be called the obedient children of God (Vs. 14). Peter declared, *"But as He who called you is holy, you also be holy in all your conduct, because it is written, 'Be holy, for I am holy'."*

That's it. The word of God, taught to us by the Holy Spirit of God, is telling us that we are to live a life of distinct holiness because the God who saved us is holy. We are to live with higher expectations than those who live in the world and live according to the lusts of their own flesh. We are to live by the declared expectations of the One whom we would call "Father".

A man came to me once and wanted my approval for getting a divorce. I asked if his wife had been unfaithful to their marriage vows. No. I asked if she had abandoned him for a life of sinful pursuits. No. I asked him if she were abusive to him. No. The upshot was that they were not on the same page as to the goals that he felt God was now calling him to pursue. They were not goals either had thought of when they were married years ago. Now he had found someone new who shared his new goals. Since the goals, he believed, had come from God (and they were goals of Christian service) then it was right before God for him to leave his first wife and pursue said goals with a new woman. He was, in fact, not in sin, according to his own point of view, since God had given him new goals and a prospective new mate to fulfill them. He would not confess that he was in sin. God couldn't have meant that that sin was for him since what he wanted to do he said was God's will. But

God has higher expectations.

Sin is defined by God, not man. God will never condone our sin just because we try to use His holy name to justify it. God has said what He meant to say. When the adulterer or homosexual comes to common confession, they can't get through it honestly unless they confesses the sin of their own practice. *"If we say we have no sin we deceive ourselves and the truth is not in us."* There is no other way to turn but to true confession of what God calls sin.

CHAPTER FOURTEEN

EVEN GREATER EXPECTATIONS

God expects His whole church to be holy. We are His people and we call Him Father. We are expected to live up to the family name. Our brother, Christ, is holy. Our Father God is holy. Our live in Helper, the Holy Spirit, is holy. We have been born again by the grace of our Holy Father. We have been washed by the blood of our Holy Brother. We are indwelt and guided by our Holy Helper. We are taught by the Holy Word. We claim membership in one holy and catholic (universal) church. God expects us to reflect the nature of our holy calling.

While God has high expectations for the whole church, there are those in the church from whom He has even higher expectations. The church uses many names and titles to identify these people. In some churches they are bishops, presbyters or elders. In others they are pastors, ministers or "reverends". In others they are called priests. The specific designation is not as important as the position and responsibilities that they hold. Whether the local church believes our holy rites or ceremonies are called sacraments or ordinances does not matter. What matters is that we believe they are specially ordained by God and to be used in His holy church for the purpose of demonstrating His truth and grace. As such they are then holy rites.

This is not only true in the New Testament era but it was also true in the Old Testament. When God gave the Law from Mount Sinai He gave instructions to Moses regarding the behavior and preparation for those who served as priest in Israel at that time. In Exodus 19:22 it says, *"Also let the priests who come near the LORD consecrate themselves, lest the LORD break out against them."* The rites of consecration for the Aaronic priesthood were given in great detail.

In Leviticus, that wonderful book that has been so maligned, great details are given about the dedication and consecration of the priest that had been chosen by God. Aaron, the brother of Moses, had been appointed by God as high priest. His sons were to work alongside him in the priestly responsibilities. One tribe of Israel, the Levites, had been chosen by God to be the servants of the priests in caring for the tabernacle and services of the Lord. The consecration rites for all of these people is given in great detail and even carries over into the next book of the Bible, Numbers.

It takes all of Leviticus chapters 8 and 9 to give the complete details of the consecration ceremony of Aaron and his sons. Then in chapter 10, after all had gone well, things went terribly wrong. Two sons of Aaron, Nadab and Abihu, having completed all the forms and rituals given to them, went a step further than commanded in defiance of God's perfect directions. Chapter 10 verse 1 says they offered *"profane fire"* before the Lord. Whether they did not use the holy incense that only priests could use as described in Exodus 30:34-38, or whether they did not use coals from the holy fire on the altar as prescribed in Leviticus 16 and already provided in Leviticus 9:24, is not known for sure. What is known is that they *"offered before the Lord which He had not commanded them."* (Leviticus 10:1)

The consequences of this action were swift and severe. Leviticus 10:2 records, *"Fire went out from the Lord and devoured them, and they died."* We don't see that happen every day, do we? All their rites and ceremonies were considered holy, and they had defiled them by choosing to do things their own way. The place in which they did it was considered a holy place and they defiled it by doing things their own way. Even the priestly garments they wore were considered holy and they defiled them by choosing to do things their own way. God wanted to set a clear precedent and example of just how holy He considered the service of worship to be. In Leviticus 10:3 God sums up His action, *"By those who come near Me I must be regarded as holy; and before all the people I must be glorified."*

What a standard God has set! By those who handle His Word and serve His people in the ministry of worship He must be regarded as holy. That means right up front that what He says is holy is holy and what He says is not holy is not holy. We have no right or position to second guess His standards. Nadab and Abihu had been two of the very few privileged ones in Exodus to spend a little time on the mountain with Moses and God. (Exodus 24:9-10) They had been formally consecrated by all the holy ceremonies that God had instituted for the priests. None of that mattered to God. In His sight they were not fit for service because they did not regard Him as holy. They had ignored His word and done their own thing and instituted their own way into His worship. They were dismissed from their jobs. Literally, they were "fired".

Years of seminary do not fit a man for the service of worship. The laying on of hands and formalities of ordination do not fit a man for the service of worship. Regarding God as holy is required to fit a man for the service or worship. Accepting His standards and not setting one's own opinions or reinterpretations of God's directions as the correct standards, is required to fit a man for the service of worship. Treating the holy declarations of God as "out of date" or "merely guidance to a primitive culture" is not meeting the requirement of regarding Him as holy. No person violating God's declared standards of morality has met the requirements of leadership in the service of worship. Though God may not pour down fire on each head as he did in Leviticus, He has no less rejected the ministry of those who defy His holiness.

There is always open the way of grace through confession, "this is a sin", and repentance, "and I will turn away from it", to everyone who would serve and worship a holy God. The hope of grace is not lost. It is more that it is just sadly ignored and abused by those who expect that His grace means that He will always look the other way. Nadab and Abihu would argue against that point. The final say will come from Jesus as He states in Matthew 7:22-23, *"Many will say to Me in that day, 'Lord, Lord, have we not prophesied in Your name, cast out demons in Your name, and done many wonders in Your name?' And then I will declare to them, 'I never knew you; depart from Me, you who practice lawlessness."*

Eight hundred years after the death of Nadab and Abihu, there was a lingering problem in Israel. Worshipping like the Canaanites had already led the northern ten tribes of Israel into captivity. Then in the very late 6th century BC God sent a final prophet to His rebellious people. Jeremiah came to warn that the final days of the land were at hand. As the rebellious priests had died before the Lord in the desert, so the rebellious priests and prophets had now led His people to destruction and exile from their land. Hear the words of Jeremiah: *"For both prophet and priest are profane; yes, in My house I have found their wickedness,"* says the LORD." (23:11) *"Also I have seen a horrible thing in the prophets of Jerusalem: They commit adultery and walk in lies; They also strengthen the hands of evildoers, so that no one turns back from his wickedness. All of them are like Sodom to Me, and her inhabitants like Gomorrah."* (23:14) *"Thus says the LORD of hosts: 'Do not listen to the words of the prophets who prophesy to you. They make you worthless; they speak a vision of their own heart, not from the mouth of the LORD'."* (23:16) *"I have not sent these prophets, yet they ran. I have not spoken to them, yet they prophesied. But if they had stood in My counsel, and had caused My people to hear My words, then they would have turned them from their evil way, and from the evil of their doings."* (23:21-22) *"Therefore behold, I am against the prophets,"* says the LORD, *"who steal*

My words everyone from his neighbor." (23:30)

God made it clear that His prophets and priests were not to practice immorality (as defined by Him) and not to speak from their own ideas. Such works and such words will not profit God's people but only lead to suffering. The prophets were to deliver the words of God and not steal them, hide them away, from the people. God wanted to heal the people, not judge them, but the prophets and priests had robbed the people of God's blessings by spouting their own ideas and living their own wicked ways, the very ways, He said, of Sodom and Gomorrah.

God's standards did not decline in the New Testament. As God gave specific details about who could serve at the altar in the Old Testament, He gave specific details about who can serve as leaders of worship today. I Timothy 3 gives one set of requirements. Here it states that the bishop is to be blameless. No one should be able to charge him with an ongoing sin as defined by Scripture. He is to have this reputation both within and without the church. He is to be self-controlled, gentle and not quarrelsome. He is also supposed to be able to teach the word of God.

When Paul gave this list of requirements to Titus he amplified this last point. In Titus 1:9 Paul stated, _"[He must] hold fast the faithful word as he has been taught that he may be able, by sound doctrine, both to exhort and convict those who contradict."_ Again we come back to the word of God as the standard. The leader of worship must be sound both in and toward the Word of God. And what word did they have in Paul's day? The New Testament was at that time in the process of being written, the letters of Paul being part of it. But by the time Paul wrote to Timothy and Titus not much except Paul's letters were available. It is quite possible that Matthew and Mark had already been finished by then as well. What they had mostly, though, was the Old Testament scriptures to learn and to teach. What Old Testament scriptures might those be? Well, Leviticus was a part of them.

Peter added a final word about leaders of the church in I Peter 5. They were to oversee the church as under-shepherds of Christ. They would give an account to Him of their service when He returned. They were, in short, to live and teach the Bible as truth as Jesus lived and taught it.

CHAPTER FIFTEEN

WHAT WOULD JESUS SAY?

After having mishandled the Old Testament teachings about homosexuality and the teachings of the Epistles about homosexuality, Mr. Thomas now turns the arrow of his contentions on the teachings of Christ. "What would Jesus do?" has become a popular cultural way of promoting just about every idea in society and even promoting products. Sadly, it is an easy mechanism to use to deceive the unknowing. The more biblically illiterate a person is the more likely they are to be duped by someone promoting whatever agenda they wish to advance. That is a real problem in contemporary American society. We have become a biblically illiterate nation.

Consider some of these statistics. As already cited, only 16% of Americans read their Bible daily[1]. That is a poor foundation for having a good knowledge of the Bible. More than 60% of Americans can't name half of the 10 Commandments or the four Gospels in the New Testament[2]. According to Barna Research Group only 40% of all Americans reported attending church weekly in 2011[3]. That was down from 49% in 1991. The Gallup Poll puts the figure closer to only 41%[4], but according to the Religious Tolerance website the actual numbers are only 21%[5]! A Harris Poll confirms the likelihood that this smaller number is more accurate[6]. Into this environment any error can be introduced without much challenge. Satan is not stupid. He knows that a vacuum can be filled and he seeks to fill it with false teaching. Jesus addressed this issue when he warned that a cleaned house needed to be filled or Satan would return and make the situation seven times worse than before. That is His description of the end of the wicked generation. (Matthew 12:43-45)

So, where does Mr. Thomas miss the mark on the teachings of Christ about homosexuality? He says that Christ is silent on the issue and then assumes that silence means it was of no great consequence to Jesus whether people were homosexuals or not. That raises two points. Was Christ silent and did Christ care?

If a person has any type of Bible reference tools (and they are inexpensive, easy to use and readily available) then they can make a quick word check and find that Christ never used the word homosexual or sodomite in his teaching. Mr. Thomas is again painting us a half truth. Mr. Thomas ignores the fact that Jesus also didn't mention many other sins. In fact, all the sins that Mr. Thomas failed to mention that are found in Leviticus 18: incest, familial co-habitation, infanticide, bestiality, etc. are also not mentioned by Jesus – at least not directly.

What Jesus did say is this, *"Do not think that I came to destroy the Law or the Prophets. I did not come to destroy but to fulfill. For assuredly, I say to you, till heaven and earth pass away, one jot or one tittle will by no means pass from the law till all is fulfilled. Whoever therefore breaks one of the least of these commandments, and teaches men so, shall be called least in the kingdom of heaven; but whoever does and teaches them, he shall be called great in the kingdom of heaven."* (Matthew 5:17-20) Heaven and earth are still here. The entire Bible is still relevant. As Jesus said, He came to fulfill the law. He did fulfill all the law. He lived a perfect life and became the sole perfect sacrifice for sin. He fulfilled all the requirements of the sacrificial, ceremonial and moral laws. At the first great church synod in Jerusalem (found in Acts 15), it is clear that the issues of ceremonial and sacrificial laws, having been fulfilled in Christ, were not binding on Gentile believers. But, the moral law was. Specifically the church synod said, *"Abstain from things offered to idols, from blood and from things strangled and from sexual immorality."* (Vs. 29) Notice the direct statement regarding sexual immorality.

Jesus Christ became the sacrifice for our sins and replaced all the sacrificial system that had only pictured His perfect sacrifice. A detailed discussion of this is found in Hebrews chapters 8-10. Certain ceremonies related to law were also fulfilled in Him and those are clearly discussed in Colossians chapter 2, most of Galatians and again in Hebrews. But in each book it is also made clear that the teachings of the moral law, Leviticus 18 as an example, were to be kept by followers of Christ. Jesus said that those who would teach anything contrary to that doctrine would not be highly esteemed by Him. The comments that Jesus related to the relevance and endurance of the Scriptures came at the beginning of the Sermon on the Mount. At the end of that Sermon He made this statement regarding those who make a mockery of His Name by using it while practicing lawlessness, *"And I will declare to them, I never knew you, depart from me you who practice lawlessness."* (Matthew 7:23)

This is not the only place, however, where Jesus discussed human sexuality. In Matthew 19:4 He says, *"Have you not read that He who made them at the beginning made them male and female."* It may seem like an innocuous enough comment, but if we look at all that God said on the point in Genesis chapter 2 we will find God's mind on the matter. (Since Jesus is God the Son, co-creator of all things, it is also His mind on the matter.) Genesis 2:18 begins God's commentary, *"And the Lord said, 'It is not good that man should be alone; I will make him a helper comparable to him."* The NIV translation uses the term *"suitable for him."* God completed this work by making a woman, not another man. Jesus, co-creator of man and woman, saw that such an arrangement was good and made note of it in the Gospels.

But Christ had hardly finished His divine comments on sexual immorality. He declared that immorality comes from the heart. *"For out of the heart proceed evil thoughts, murders, adulteries, fornications, thefts, false witness and blasphemies."* (Matthew 15:19) We have seen where this is the common nature of mankind. The word in this verse translated fornications has a broad New Testament meaning. It does not only mean pre-marital sex, it also includes the idea of any illicit sexual intercourse and is "metaphorically associated with pagan idolatry.[7]" And what does this bring us back to? It brings us back full circle to the Canaanite religious practices that included all the various forms of sexual immorality as discussed in Leviticus 18 including homosexual behavior.

The book of Mark gives a clear statement of Jesus on the subject of the evilness of the heart of man. In addition to the comments on adultery and fornication used in Matthew 15, Mark included the broader commentary of Jesus on the topic of sexual immorality. In Mark 7:22 Jesus explained His use of adultery and fornication. He used the word "lewdness" (NKJV) or "lasciviousness" (KJV). The Greek word used here is variously translated in the King James New Testament as lasciviousness, filthy and wantonness. In I Peter 4:3 the word is attached to the phrase "abominable idolatries" (NKJV) and reflects the nature of the acts as related to pagan religious practices. Again we see the condemnation of the sins of Canaan. In II Peter 2:7 the word is used in conjunction with the acts of the people of Sodom and Gomorrah which have already been proven to be homosexual in nature. Peter also pointed out in II Peter 2:2 that the church would come to a time when false teachers would promote these false doctrines as true and bring into disrepute the whole gospel of Christ. Jude used the Greek word to describe how false teachers would preach such sexual lewdness as truth to the destruction of the church and the damnation of their own souls. So, when Jesus used this word as the nature of man in Mark 7:22 He was not speaking lightly but was addressing the very sexual sins that today are so corrupting the truth of His word and the sound doctrine of His church.

Jesus, very much to the contrary of Mr. Thomas's assertion, did address homosexuality and He did it clearly.

Mr. Thomas had wanted us to believe that Jesus never commented on homosexuality. He was correct that Jesus never used the term. That was only a half, and very misleading, half-truth. Jesus did comment repeatedly on the subject of the accuracy and relevance of all the Law and the Prophets. We have seen that they were uniform in their denunciation of the practice. He said that we must teach that law and not follow the dictates of our own sinful and immoral hearts. He said that God made woman for man. Dear friend, Jesus taught a lot on homosexuality.

He didn't harp on it, of course. That wasn't His purpose for being here to just kick around those trapped in sin. He knew everyone was trapped in sin. He came to fix the problem, not just condemn it. Luke 19:10 tells us *"for the Son of Man has come to seek and to save that which was lost."* Jesus knew the depravity of man and He spoke honestly and openly about it. He never condoned sin in anyone. But Jesus came with a remedy.

His purpose was far greater than that of the Old Testament prophets including John the Baptist. What was their message? Repent, repent, repent! Jesus did teach repentance. Mark declared in chapter 1:15 that repentance was part of His message. But it wasn't the bulk of His message. When He called for repentance He also called for belief in the Good News, the gospel, that God had sent His Son to redeem mankind. He called for mankind to leave the darkness of sin and to walk in the light of His light.

Did Jesus care about sin? Immensely so! How much did He care? He died for sinners. That is showing a great deal of care. Did He die so that sinners could continue to live in the practice of sin from which His death was to free them? No! As Paul said in Romans 6:1-2, *"Shall we continue in sin that grace may abound? God forbid!"*

Jesus' message to sinners was that they must be born again.

John related in John 3:3, *"Jesus answered and said to him, "Most assuredly, I say to you, unless one is born again, he cannot see the kingdom of God."* The New Testament relates being born again to a grain of wheat. The seed planted does not look like the plant that comes up. The new life is different from the old.

A group of hypocritical Jews brought a woman to Jesus. She had been caught in adultery, they said. In the very act, they said. According to Jewish law the man was guilty as well. They didn't bring him. This hypocrisy was not lost on Jesus. After the false accusers had all left, Jesus made two comments to the woman. First He told her that He did not condemn her. She wasn't going to die for this sin. Then He told her something else. *"Go and sin no more."* (John 8:11) What He said is, "I have saved you, now change your behavior." That is what He says to every sinner who comes to Him. The new birth will bring forth the fruit of new behavior. It is that simple.

Jesus is concerned about all sinful behaviors. He openly condemned them without the need to mention each specific one. He died to deliver us from the dread consequences of our sins. He called us to new birth, a new life walking in His light and not the old call of the flesh. Yes, Jesus is concerned enough to have given us both the warning and the way. Amen.

CHAPTER SIXTEEN

ANOTHER HALF-TRUTH

Mr. Thomas now wants to quote another verse of the New Testament to gain an advantage that God does not give him. We are admonished by the Scriptures, he points out, to judge not[1]. What he tries to make of that point is that it is the weight of the teaching of Jesus Christ. It is, figuratively, to be the final stake driven through the heart of all the bloodsucking anti-sodomites. But is it?

Certainly Satan has distorted the meaning of this Scripture more times than can be numbered. Here he tries it again. Satan doesn't want sin to be called sin. He wants the church to be afraid of speaking out against the profanities of the world. Only hate mongers would do that, he insinuates. Good people "judge not". The result is that the church, believing Satan more than God, goes on its dysfunctional way allowing sin to seep deeper and deeper into its midst. Where are the likes of Paul who stood up and boldly said in I Corinthians 6:9-10, *"Do you not know that the unrighteous will not inherit the kingdom of God? Do not be deceived. Neither fornicators, nor idolaters, nor adulterers, nor homosexuals, nor sodomites, nor thieves, nor covetous, nor drunkards, nor revilers, nor extortioners will inherit the kingdom of God."* What about Jude who writes in Jude 3-4, *"I found it necessary to write to you exhorting you to contend earnestly for the faith which was once for all delivered to the saints.*

For certain men have crept in unnoticed, who long ago were marked out for this condemnation, ungodly men, who turn the grace of our God into lewdness and deny the only Lord God and our Lord Jesus Christ."

Were Paul and Jude judging or were they declaring the known word of God? Is to say what God has already said judging? That would be preposterous. Remember that Mr. Thomas is a lawyer. Every day in every court lawyers and judges cite case law that comes from earlier judgments. They are not judging. They are simply stating the facts. Mr. Thomas knows that is true but avoids that inconvenient truth in presenting his cause. If the Supreme Court has decided something, then it is not judging to cite their judgment. If God has said something, then it is not judging to say what He has said. Sin is sin and God has set the laws regarding it. Satan would have us to believe that to do so is judging. Satan is a liar. (John 8:44)

Let us take just a brief moment, before we get back to the comments from Christ about dealing with sin in the church, to examine what judging really is. Romans 14 is a great guide for us. In verses 3 and 4 Paul began to present the case about judging. *"Let not him who eats despise him who does not eat, and let not him who does not eat judge him who eats; for God has received him. Who are you to judge another's servant? To his own master he stands or falls. Indeed, he will be made to stand, for God is able to make him stand."* Some people in the church liked to practice fasting as a sign of religious devotion. Others did not. Paul went on in the chapter to point out that some people observed special holy days while others did not. Again there was the admonishment to not judge each other.

Let us employ a modern example. Lent is a season of the church in some denominations and is not a season of the church in others. Since Lent can be both about fasting and observing of days, it is a practical example of Paul's comments. Here is what could be said by the people who do practice Lent concerning those who don't. "Don't those fools understand the importance of devotion to God in penance and prayer? Don't they care about cleaning up their lives and setting their devotion more fully on God?" Those two accusations, of course, are judgments about the spirituality of others. Those not practicing Lent might argue back in like fashion. "What are those fools doing? They certainly don't understand that Jesus paid it all and that we have no need for self-humiliation today. They are unlearned and superstitious and expect to get God to notice them for all their deeds." These people also are judging.

Paul's point in Romans 14 is that God will be the judge of the motives and spiritual exercises of His saints. Whether they eat or don't eat; whether they observe a day or don't observe a day; they do it all to God. Whatever is done as a service to Christ, either in abstention or consumption, is between the believer and God. If the motives are wrong then God will judge. It is the fact that people are devoting themselves to God that is important in either case. Paul concluded the passage like this in verses 12 and 13, *"So then each of us shall give account of himself to God. Therefore let us not judge one another anymore, but rather resolve this, not to put a stumbling block or a cause to fall in our brother's way."*

We have far too many such cases dividing the church of Jesus Christ. Earlier I mentioned a common confessional creed used in some denominations. In those churches there is a time of "common confession" of sin where a prayer and corporate confession is made. In other churches there is no such thing. Common confessions are viewed by many, in the latter churches, as "hollow gestures." Those who make common confessions could retaliate that the others must not think that confession and cleansing is important. Both would be judgments. Both groups could worship much more happily together if they could get by their biases and not judge each other's motives before God. The same could be said of the recitation of the Apostles' Creed or the praying of the Lord's Prayers. The use or disuse of them is not a matter for judgment from one believer to the other. They are deeply personal issues of worship toward God and He will judge the motive and intent of each action and receive the worship that is truly His.

This is what "false judgment" is all about. God calls us to worship Him. All believers have a desire to obey this command. Each, however, may bring a different dimension to this worship. Judging another's motive in worship is opening us up to judgment about our own true worship and devotion. Let us make sure that we are right in that and then rejoice in God.

But there are things we cannot bring to our worship of God. They are things that He has already declared to be sin. My wife and I can worship God in our sexual relationship. We can honor Him in our fidelity and obedience to His word. The fornicator, the adulterer, the incestual, the pornographer and the homosexual cannot worship God in their sexual relationships. God has already judged their sins and called them unclean before Him. For the church to proclaim the same message is not judgment. For the church not to proclaim these practices as the sin that God calls them is to weaken the message of God's authority and to undermine the relevance of the church in society. If the church doesn't know right from wrong, how will anyone else?

That brings us back again to the actual teachings of Christ concerning sin in the church. These are found in Matthew 18:15-18, *"Moreover if your brother sins against you, go and tell him his fault between you and him alone. If he hears you, you have gained your brother. But if he will not hear, take with you one or two more, that 'by the mouth of two or three witnesses every word may be established.' And if he refuses to hear them, tell it to the church. But if he refuses even to hear the church, let him be to you like a heathen and a tax collector. Assuredly, I say to you, whatever you bind on earth will be bound in heaven, and whatever you loose on earth will be loosed in heaven."* When there is sexual immorality in the church, that sin must be confronted and dealt with. It is not a matter of judging motives. It is a matter of declaring that the Church belongs to God and He has standards for it.

In ancient Israel God told the people that if someone was

caught transgressing the laws that He had given that those people were to be cut off by the rest from the worship of the sanctuary. Over 20 times in the Law God declares that He will cut off those people who practice various sins from the congregation of Israel. He also declared that the people of God were to participate in cutting them off. In some cases it was by death and in others it was by keeping them from corporate worship with God. God also pointed out that if the congregation would not do their part in cutting off certain people from worship, that He would still do it Himself. The consequence, however, would be that all the people would become polluted by the sin that they had tolerated and then they would corporately bear the punishment. God takes the holiness of His people and the holiness of His worship very seriously.

God does not call for us to kill anyone today within the church. God does call us, however, to deal with sin within the church. To stand in the pulpit and say "this is sin" is not a violation of the admonition to judge not. God has already judged. To be silent about sin is a much greater spiritual travesty. In the church at Corinth there was sexual sin of such a degree that Paul said even the Gentiles would be ashamed to practice it. And how did the church react? They let it be. Paul said to them, *"And you are puffed up, and have not rather mourned, that he who has done this deed might be taken away from among you. Your glorying is not good. Do you not know that a little leaven leavens the whole lump? Therefore purge out the old leaven."* (I Corinthians 5:2, 6&7) Paul was obeying the teachings of Christ in Matthew 18. He was not violating anything said by Christ in Matthew 7:1 about judging not. The sin was egregious and had already been condemned by God. He was simply telling the truth.

The message to the church is very simple. Don't be silenced by Satan. In the Garden of Eden he misused God's word in his deception of Eve. In the wilderness temptation of Christ he came to the Son of God and tried again to employ his old tricks of misusing God's word. Jesus didn't fall for it and remained sinless. Now Christ's call to us is not to be duped by Satan and his tricks. Satan, that old serpent, has already been judged and to say so is not judging; it is just speaking the truth. The practice of sin has already been defined by God and to say so is not judging; it is simple obedience to our Creator and Savior Jesus Christ.

CHAPTER SEVENTEEN

JUDGE NOT WITH HYPOCRISY

As we have seen, when Jesus said to "judge not" in Matthew 7, He had a lot more to say than most people want to consider. That He was not talking about judging sin as sin has been clearly shown. But when we do judge sin as sin, then there is something to be considered as well. Jesus said in the total quote on "judge not" in Matthew 7:1-5, *"Judge not, that you be not judged. For with what judgment you judge, you will be judged; and with the measure you use, it will be measured back to you. And why do you look at the speck in your brother's eye, but do not consider the plank in your own eye? Or how can you say to your brother, 'Let me remove the speck from your eye'; and look, a plank is in your own eye? Hypocrite! First remove the plank from your own eye, and then you will see clearly to remove the speck from your brother's eye."*

Does the visible church already have a "plank" of sexual sin in its midst that needs to be repented of and from which we must move to a more biblical standard of practice? The question has been asked and answered repeatedly. Is homosexual practice a sin? The answer from God is an emphatic YES! Is homosexual practice the only sexual sin? The answer from God is an emphatic, NO! Is the church of Jesus Christ as vocal in its condemnation of other sexual sin as it is of homosexuality? The answer is probably, not so much. Even in churches which have stood staunchly against homosexual behavior, other immoral behaviors have become more tolerated. This is the plank in the church's eye. James, the brother of Christ, has something to say on this important issue. *"For whoever shall keep the whole law, and yet stumble in one point, he is guilty of all. For He who said, 'Do not commit adultery,' also said, 'Do not murder.' Now if you do not commit adultery, but you do murder, you have become a transgressor of the law."* (James 2:10-11)

The church that would never allow in homosexuals will hardly bat an eye anymore at adulterers or fornicators or pornographers. According to surveys up to 50% or more of church leaders view pornography and admit that it is a problem in their home[1]. The same sad statistics aren't just for pastors. The men in the pews have the same practices. According to James if we break part of the law we have broken the whole thing. The point would be not to stop condemning homosexuality as a sin, but it would be to both preach and practice that pornography is a sin as well.

High profile cases of leading evangelicals involved in immorality draw even greater scrutiny than the overwhelming statistics concerning church leaders and pornography. That practice is maybe too common to attract headlines. But headlines are made on an all too regular basis by those who have spoken one thing from the pulpit and practiced another altogether in their private life. From Jimmy Swaggart in 1986 to today, the media have reported the failure of conservative evangelical Christian leaders to practice what they preached. When Christian mega-media ministries make a lot of noise about sexual purity, the world is watching to see if it means what it says. The Christian community has invited the spotlight by making such earnest appeals to the world to change their behaviors that the world wants to know if we have changed ours.

But if we set aside the headline stories and statistical studies, there are greater issues of tolerance of sexual immorality in our churches than ever before. Let us consider fornication as just one area. There are 4 key Greek words that are translated fornication or harlot or variations of these two terms. Those words are used 56 times in the New Testament. That is a lot of teaching on that topic and it appears in the Gospels, the Epistles and Revelation. And what is fornication? The Merriam-Webster Dictionary definition is, "consensual sexual intercourse between two persons not married to each other."[2] This can, of course, then also include adultery and prostitution.

Just using the main definition and not including adultery and prostitution, how is this seen today? Years ago the term "shacking up" was employed. Now couples simply opt to live together without the benefit of marriage. In many cases, though, they don't even live together. Sex is just another item on the menu of their life. According to the BBC the number of children born outside of a married family increased from 12% of all babies in 1980 to 42% in 2004[3]. Those numbers are mirrored in the Unites States. According to Child Trends DataBank[4], the number of single mother births in the Unites States in 2011 was 41%.

Does the visible church mirror these statistics? While it is hard to find any kind of specific statistic on this issue, the observant person will have to say, "Yes". Is any call made any longer for public repentance for this sexual immorality? So many people in the church have accepted this as an unstoppable trend that the mere suggestion of a call for public repentance is considered to be a brutal act of public shaming. I do realize that some churches still do require an act of public confession for such behaviors, but the visible church has largely abandoned the practice. Still, much of the visible church condemns immoral practice in others outside the church body. Jesus said to let our judgment be without hypocrisy.

Adultery is another area of conduct that has lost its stigma in the visible church. Adultery in the Greek appears in 5 related words. Those words appear 35 times in the New Testament.

Like fornication they appear in the Gospels, Epistles and Revelation. Most importantly adultery is prohibited by the 7th commandment. Yet with all this condemnation of the practice in Scripture there is less and less censure of the practice in the visible church today.

In Matthew 19:9 Jesus said that divorce lead to the double practice of adultery. *"And I say to you, whoever divorces his wife, except for sexual immorality, and marries another, commits adultery; and whoever marries her who is divorced commits adultery."* According to divorcestatistics.org the rate of divorce for first time marriages in the United States is 45-50%. For second marriages it is nearly 2 out of 3 and for third marriages it is 70%[5]. Is the church immune to this violation of holy matrimony? No. Do many churches go right on marrying people into new adulterous relationships? Yes. Has the visible church failed to uphold the sanctity of marriage? Largely so. The visible church needs to take a stand on the sanctity of marriage and the commission of adultery. It needs to uphold the teaching of its Lord and Savior Jesus Christ and mend its broken promises of fidelity to Him.

There are two other conservative views also taken concerning divorce. Paul stated in I Corinthians 7:15 that if an unbeliever departed, the believing partner was now free. *"But if the unbeliever departs, let him depart; a brother or a sister is not under bondage in such cases."* This may convey the meaning of spiritual immorality. If the unbelieving depart then they have chosen the love of the god of this world to love of spouse and that spouses' love of the Creator and Savior of the world. This situation is the word abandonment. Another reason is sometimes put forth as just cause for divorce. It is based on the Old Testament statute that entitled a slave to have his freedom if he or she were to be abusively injured by his master. (Exodus 21:26-27) There is a far greater responsibility for spousal kindness than for that of master to servant. (I Peter 3:1-7) So the abused may depart without sinning. These three A's are a conservative, but not universal, standard: Abandonment, Abuse and Adultery. They provide an opportunity for those who have gone through an affliction of sin to move on in a state of holy matrimony. Good premarital counseling, in such cases, and the wedding of a sincere believer in Jesus Christ offer hope for the future of those whose marriages have been destroyed by sin.

Many times I hear people sigh and say, "Oh, the world is getting to be such a wicked place. I wish Jesus would hurry and come back." I have even heard openly lost people challenge God by saying, "Why doesn't Jesus come back and set all of this straight if He is such a loving God?" My friend, if Jesus came back right now it is the church who would be in a great deal of trouble. Amos, the prophet, told us Amos 4:18, *"Woe to you who desire the day of the LORD! For what good is the day of the LORD to you?"* The day of the Lord's appearing will not be joyful to those who live in constant rebellion to His word. Peter told us this in I Peter 4:17-18, *"For the time has come for judgment to begin at the house of God; and if it begins with us first, what will be the end of those who do not obey the gospel of God? Now, 'If the righteous one is scarcely saved, where will the ungodly and the sinner appear?'"*

It is time for judgment to come to the house of God. It is time that the house of God begins to judge itself. As part of the great admonition for properly coming to the Table of the Lord, Paul said to us in I Corinthians 11:31, *"For if we would judge ourselves, we would not be judged."* The church needs to guard itself on being the great judge of one sin only. Sexual immorality is blight on the character of the Church of Jesus Christ. God told the Israelites that if they practiced the sins of Canaan that He would judge them. That message has been passed along to the church by Peter. The visible church is standing in increasing opposition to the one whom it calls Lord. Repentance needs to begin with the house of God. Our moral crimes against Christ cannot be covered by a loud denunciation of the moral crimes that others commit. The church needs to seriously deal with the "plank" in its own eye and remove that hypocrisy from our judgment.

CHAPTER EIGHTEEN

PUT THEM ALL TO DEATH!

The Bible is a wonderful book. It is a real book in that it deals with things in an honest state of reality. Abraham sinned. David sinned. Moses sinned. Peter sinned. That is reality. The Bible doesn't sugar coat the truth. It includes seemingly horrid stories of rape, incest, murder, intrigue and the like in harsh and stark honesty. People live sinful lives. That reveals the great need of mankind. We need to have our sins forgiven. It is the great gift of God that He has given us forgiveness in the blood of His Son Jesus Christ. What is often and sadly overlooked in the act of forgiveness is the call to "put to death" the old man of sin within us whose corruption had earned us the just condemnation of the holy God. It is by this standard that we judge ourselves.

This brings us to a biblical account that causes some uneasiness in the lost or spiritually untrained community. God mandated that the children of Israel should utterly destroy all the inhabitants of the land of Canaan leaving none that breathed alive. People falsely accuse God of harshness or cruelty in passing this judgment on the Canaanites. Nobody seems particularly upset that David slew Goliath who had been busy for 40 days denouncing God. These same people are not terribly upset that the evil men who conspired against Daniel and had him thrown into the den of lions should have experienced that fate themselves. They are also not overly anxious about the death of all the firstborn in Egypt or the vast Egyptian army that died in the Red Sea chasing down the Israelites. But this group of people gets particularly upset by God's command to destroy all that breathed in Canaan.

A little honesty here would not hurt. Goliath sinned and was killed. The evil counselors in Daniel sinned and were killed. Pharaoh had spurned God's grace repeatedly and so his armies were killed. There is a consistent cause and effect relationship here. Sin brings death. So it was for the Canaanites. Their sin was egregious. They committed every conceivable sexual sin. They practiced routine infanticide. They mocked God's power with every idol they erected and every sacrifice they made to those idols. They had exchanged the glory of God for the fantasies of their own minds. They had shed much innocent blood and performed multiple abominations.

They had done all this after the clear testimony among them of people like Abraham, Isaac and Jacob. They had ignored great leaders like the righteous Melchizedek who had reigned in their midst. They had ignored the preaching of righteous Lot, although those particular Canaanites had already faced a fiery death. Even in the midst of the judgment on their sinful brothers, the Canaanites had not repented or changed a thing. They had only grown more wicked. God had given them 400 years from the time of Abraham to repent, but they rejected that opportunity until their iniquity became so complete that there was nothing left for them but death. God had prophesied just such a course of events to Abraham in Genesis 15 concluding with this comment about the Canaanites in verse 16, *"But in the fourth generation they (the children of Abraham) shall return here (from a nation that has afflicted them), for the iniquity of the Amorites is not yet complete."*

God had been patient with the Amorites, part of the Canaanite people group, for four hundred years. That is a long time of patience before sin is judged. But instead of responding to righteous teaching the people had only grown worse until their sin was fully ripe or complete. The destruction of the Canaanites was just punishment for their total wickedness.

The issue was that Israel was going to live in the land. God called the practices of the Amorites abominations. God did not want His children to live with those whose practices were abominable lest His children also learned to do such utter wickedness. The land, as we have seen from Leviticus 18 had been fully polluted with the sins of Canaan. The land itself was sick of the disease of their sin. For the sake of the land and the preservation of His people God had to expel the Canaanites completely. No injustice was done as there were no innocents in the land. The command of God was clear as seen in Deuteronomy 20:17-18, *"But you shall utterly destroy them: the Hittite and the Amorite and the Canaanite and the Perizzite and the Hivite and the Jebusite, just as the LORD your God has commanded you, lest they teach you to do according to all their abominations which they have done for their gods, and you sin against the LORD your God."* God wanted the land purified for the sake of His people.

The same principle is found in the New Testament. In the New Testament God does not have a "land". We cannot say that this place or that place is God's land as could be said of the Promised Land in the Old Testament. Israel is still the Promised Land of the Jews, but God's people today are called by the Name of His Son Jesus Christ. Christians have no land of their own. Paul made this clear in Philippians 3:20, *"For our citizenship is in heaven, from which we also eagerly wait for the Savior, the Lord Jesus Christ."* Also the author of Hebrews said in Hebrews 13:14, *"For here we have no continuing city, but we seek the one to come."* In the New Testament God does not dwell with His people in a land, He dwells with His people wherever they are. Each individual Christian is the dwelling place of God. Paul said in II Corinthians 6:19, *"Or do you not know that your body is the temple of the Holy Spirit who is in you, whom you have from God, and you are not your own?"*

We who believe in Jesus Christ are now His "land". He has taken up residence in us. That is a great and wonderful act of grace. Without abrogating His promise of territorial Israel to the Jewish people, for the gifts and calling of God are without repentance (Romans 11:29), God has expanded His dwelling to be within the people of His church worldwide. He has become what He told Isaiah that He would become in Isaiah 54:5, *"For your Maker is your husband, the LORD of hosts is His name; and your Redeemer is the Holy one of Israel; He is called the God of the whole earth."* He is the God of the whole earth.

Now, what God wanted in the Land of Israel is what God wants in His new temple, the church. He wanted a clean, unpolluted land. He wanted the Canaanites to be gone. He wanted the Israelites to worship Him in holiness. They failed to do this on many levels. They failed to obey Him and destroy the Canaanites. They failed to obey Him and not practice Canaanite religious perversions. They failed to heed the voices of the prophets sent to return them to God. They failed to read and study the Word that had been given to them and which they were commanded to read and know and pass on to their children. (Deuteronomy 6:6-9) Thus their land became polluted once again with all the immoralities of Canaan and God was faithful to His word and removed from them the protective grace of His love.

God calls the church today, each individual member of it, to do what Israel did not do. He calls us to put to death **the sins** of Canaan. No, He doesn't call us to put to death the Canaanites. We, our sinful nature, are the Canaanites. We are the practitioners of all abominations in our heart against God. We are the ones condemned to die for our sinful estate. Paul said in Ephesians 2:1-3, *"And you, **who were dead** in trespasses and sins, in which you once walked according to the course of this world, according to the prince of the power of the air, the spirit who now works in the sons of disobedience, among whom also we all once conducted ourselves* *in the lusts of our flesh, fulfilling the desires of the flesh and of the mind, and were **by nature children of wrath**, just as the others."*

Our nature was death and our end was the wrath of God just like the Canaanites. But God intervened through Jesus Christ and bought us as His very own. By faith we came to Him for forgiveness of our vile affections and to be called His children. Now He wants His children to be what they were always meant to be. He wants us to be holy and living testimonies of His grace and love like Israel was supposed to do when He freed them from Egypt.

To do this we need to put to death the old man, the Canaanite in all of us. Paul said in Colossians 3:5-6, *"Therefore* **put to death** *your members which are on the earth: fornication, uncleanness, passion, evil desire, and covetousness, which is idolatry. Because of these things the wrath of God is coming upon the sons of disobedience."* He told us to put to death the very things listed in Leviticus 18 that had polluted the land and that God does not want in our land. Paul also stated in Romans 8:13, *"For if you live according to the flesh you will die; but if by the Spirit you put to death the deeds of the body, you will live."*

Our warfare is not warfare of swords and spears but a spiritual battle that must be fought daily. The old man is our flesh. Our flesh remains with us until we die. The lusts and desires of the flesh remain with us all our lives. Our warfare is spiritual. The Holy Spirit who now lives within us alerts our conscience, which is clean through Christ, to the call of our flesh which is contrary to the holiness of God's call upon us. Galatians 5:16-17 says, *"I say then: Walk in the Spirit, and you shall not fulfill the lust of the flesh. For the flesh lusts against the Spirit, and the Spirit against the flesh; and these are contrary to one another, so that you do not do the things that you wish."*

Here is our standard of measurement for self-judgment. How am I doing at being the "land of God"? Do I let the Canaanite within me run his foul course or am I vigilant to guard against the demon idols of flesh and desire that he craves? Do I appreciate the salvation of Jesus Christ and am I glad that He saved me from what I was? While never fully succeeding (see all of Romans chapter 7), am I never-the-less trying to let my body be a holy temple for God? This is our avenue for judgment. Do I judge myself to be putting to death the old man or not?

CHAPTER NINETEEN

GOD WILL JUDGE OUTSIDERS

In case anyone is concerned that those outside the church get a free ride while the church is cleaning its own house, this is simply not the case. Nowhere does God imply that sin will be ignored. His holy standard applies to the saved believer in Jesus Christ and to the rebellious Canaanite as well. God judged Canaan for all their wickedness. He didn't say to Israel, "Now don't you do those things or I will judge you, but they can get away with it because they are not mine." No, God judged Canaan and wanted Israel to completely exterminate them. They were a pestilence to the land and a foul odor in the nostrils of a holy God. They were and they still are.

Paul wrote in I Corinthians 5:12-13 specific comments concerning our realm of judgment and God's. *"For what have I to do with judging those also who are outside? Do you not judge those who are inside?* ___But those who are outside God judges___. *Therefore 'put away from yourselves the evil person'."* The final comment of the verse is a reference to Deuteronomy 17:7 and the need for Israel to judge and punish those within their nation who were guilty of sin. God would take care of the world; they were to take care of their own sins using God's standard. Both statements are true regarding the church and the world today.

Our Apostles' Creed recognizes the judging power of God

over all the earth. The second frame of the Creed concludes, "From thence He shall come to judge the quick and the dead." The New Testament applies this to duty to both God the Son and God the Father. (Acts 10:42 and Hebrews 10:23) Revelation 20 details the final judgment of God. Revelation 20:11-15 says, *"Then I saw a great white throne and Him who sat on it, from whose face the earth and the heaven fled away. And there was found no place for them. And I saw the dead, small and great, standing before God, and books were opened. And another book was opened, which is the Book of Life. And the dead were judged according to their works, by the things which were written in the books. The sea gave up the dead who were in it, and Death and Hades delivered up the dead who were in them. And they were judged, each one according to his works. Then Death and Hades were cast into the lake of fire. This is the second death. And anyone not found written in the Book of Life was cast into the lake of fire."*

At this same time there will be many who have boasted of their name being in the Book of Life but of whom Jesus will say, *"Many will say to Me in that day, 'Lord, Lord, have we not prophesied in Your name, cast out demons in Your name, and done many wonders in Your name?' And then I will declare to them, 'I never knew you; depart from Me, you who practice lawlessness!'"* (Matt 7:22-23) This does not bode well for all those who think that the practice of homosexuality is somehow OK with God. They can use all the normal forms of worship and creed, perform all the outward services of worship, but their constant rebellion to the truth of God's word will pay negative dividends in the end. Jesus will say, "Depart from me; I never knew you. You have practiced lawlessness. You have said that My word was no good and opted to choose your own words and ways instead." Again He may quote to them those powerful words from Leviticus 10:3, *"By those who come near Me I must be regarded as holy; and before all the people I must be glorified."* With those words God poured out a fiery judgment on the sons of Aaron. With similar words God the Father and the Son will pour out fiery judgment on those who make a public mockery of His Word and consequently the

Name of Jesus.

Thus far we have only considered future judgment. All judgment, however, is not just in the future. We can go back to Genesis and see that the judgment of God can be very present. There is the case of Sodom and Gomorrah. In a nearby region of Salem lived Melchizedek who is defined in Hebrews 7:2 as being *"king of righteousness and king of peace."* We know from Genesis 14 that the King of Sodom knew this man. The King of Sodom also knew Abraham. Abraham was the friend of God. In the city of Sodom lived a man named Lot. The New Testament tells us that Lot was a righteous man, a man who would have warned them of their wickedness. The citizens of Sodom even accused him of acting like a judge on their deeds. (Gen. 19:9) Indeed, Lot's soul was abused by their immorality every day. (II Peter 2:7)The city had not lived without warning of its sinfulness. Finally God acted. The city was consumed with fiery judgment.

In the book of Exodus we again find the present judgment of God. Egypt had offered haven to the family of Joseph in Genesis 45. By Exodus 1 they had turned to the abuse of God's people. The moral abuse that Lot had felt in Sodom was physical and spiritual abuse in Egypt. God had given the Amorites 400 years to repent after the burning of Sodom. During those 400 years Israel had dwelt in Egypt and suffered abuse there. The Egyptians had the witness of God in their midst. They had the memory of the salvation of their nation provided by Joseph through the wisdom and power of God. But like Sodom, Egypt had ignored the witness of truth they had received. So God raised up a Pharaoh to demonstrate His power and judgment on that nation. (Exodus 9:16) And God did judge them mightily. The nation was ruined financially through plague after plague. There was agricultural destruction. There were health plagues, a death sentence on the first born and finally military defeat.

Going on we find the judgment of God against the

Canaanites recorded in Numbers and Joshua. In the first six years or so of the war (including the war against Sihon and Og in the land east of the Jordan River) the Israelites were faithful to exterminate everyone except the Gibeonites. Afterwards they became less diligent in obeying God and ultimately paid the price by facing God's judgment themselves. In the book of Numbers we also find multiple instances of God's present judgment on Israel. The ground opened up and swallowed the rebellious Dathan and his entire family. (Numbers 16) Fire came down and consumed the rebellious Korah and his followers. (Numbers 16) Fiery serpents were sent by God to punish the rebels in Numbers 21. Those who called themselves by God's name but lived in rebellion fared no better than the Canaanites in the judgment of God.

Both instant and progressive judgment of God is recorded in the remainder of the Old Testament and in the New Testament as well. Saul lost his kingship for rebellion. Solomon had his kingdom divided in the days of his son due to his marriage of pagan women and practicing Canaanite religions. Sennacherib, King of Assyria – the mightiest nation on earth at that time, mocked God. In one night God slew in their sleep 185,000 soldiers of the king's army. In disgrace he returned to his own land and was assassinated by his own sons. Nebuchadnezzar, the great king of Babylon, the next mighty nation on earth, bragged of his own accomplishments and was driven from civilization to live as a beast. The entire northern 10 tribes of Israel followed in the footsteps of the Canaanites and their abominations and were conquered and dispersed by Assyria. Judah failed to heed God's warnings through the prophets and the destruction of the Northern Kingdom and was carried away captive by the Babylonians.

God was patient in each case. In each case He had sent a messenger to warn the offenders of their sins. In each case the warnings were ignored. In each case judgment was sure. Jesus warned the Jews that if they did not believe in Him they would face the destruction of their homeland within a generation. Within forty years of Christ's crucifixion the city of Jerusalem was overrun by the Roman army in a most merciless suppression of their rebellion. God always warns and then God will always act. The New Living Translation puts Amos 3:7 like this, *"But always, first of all, I warn you through my servants the prophets. I, the Sovereign LORD, have now done this."* Patient warning and then action is the pattern of God's judgment.

Not all the judgments of God have been as dramatic as Sodom and Gomorrah. Egypt, though judged, is still there. Babylon was judged for what they did to Judah, but Babylon was still an important city at the time of Christ and nation of Iraq, modern Babylon, has caused trouble even to this day. Israel was twice removed from their land but they are back today. Still, they face daily hostility and aggression from both the Palestinians and neighboring countries. It is not a peaceful return to the land. Most of the judgments of God in history have been partial in nature to produce repentance. All, however, exist to point to the fact of the final judgment and of the power of God to fulfill it.

Do we see the judgment of God today? Absolutely! Do we recognize the judgment of God today? Generally we do not. Pharaoh was unimpressed by many of God's judgments against him. He attributed some to the same demonic powers his priests used. Judah and Israel both ignored the repeated cycles of judgment of God that came upon them. Their false prophets tried to give the events of the day a natural explanation that could not include the anger of God. God railed against the false prophets for leading His people astray with their own false opinions, visions, of what was going on. The same is true of today.

We as a nation have moved past any spiritual understanding. The Bible is summarily discounted as an "old book" of "old ideas." We are more mature in our understanding of the world around us and the "natural order of things". Droughts, vicious storms and earthquakes cannot have a spiritual meaning because the spirit world is really just mythology. We do not wish to see God active in raising up politicians who bring His judgments on corrupt nations, ours included. We do not want to admit that economic events can have spiritual connections. This type of smug rejection of God is even common in church circles. We have come to desire only a "Santa Claus" god who only does nice things. Where the word of God has been dismissed as irrelevant, the actions of God must also be dismissed as being the result of other causes. But make no mistake. God is judging the nations and America is not exempt.

CHAPTER TWENTY

GOD'S INDICTMENT AND RIGHTEOUS JUDGMENT

Rampant pornography and homosexuality and sexual indecency of every sort brought the judgment of God on Canaan and will do so to any modern society as well. Nations cannot murder their unborn with impunity in the eyes of God. The Canaanites murdered their babies in a sacrifice to their gods. Modern nations let women sacrifice their babies to the god of self. Indecency was the norm in Canaan and became so in Israel. Homosexuality is becoming a protected status in the modern American culture. Our own president applauds those who "come out of the closet". Shame and possible criminal charges are brought against those who speak out against it. To speak against these sins in ancient nations was to bring rebuke from both religious and government authorities whose vested interest was to preserve the status quo of the day and not worry about future problems from God.

But problems are not future. They are present. America has the highest death rate by violent crime of any developed country in the world. Global warming, or the new name, global climate change, is blamed for many acts that God has used in the past to judge nations. Changes came in climate patterns in all of history in response to God's divine judgment on nations. Today is it then just a natural occurrence? Sweeping plagues of illness are recorded as acts of God's judgment. Are they today just the result of too many antibiotics being used? Financial ruin has come as a consequence of God's wrath throughout history. Are today's financial woes just the result of poor government oversight or of government's own abuse of finances?

God indicts man by His righteous judgment in Romans 1:28-32. It reads like a listing of headlines in today's newspapers. *"And even as they did not like to retain God in their knowledge, God gave them over to a debased mind, to do those things which are not fitting; being filled with all unrighteousness, sexual immorality, wickedness, covetousness, maliciousness; full of envy, murder, strife, deceit, evil-mindedness; they are whisperers, backbiters, haters of God, violent, proud, boasters, inventors of evil things, disobedient to parents, undiscerning, untrustworthy, unloving, unforgiving, unmerciful; who, knowing the righteous judgment of God, that those who practice such things are deserving of death, not only do the same but also approve of those who practice them."*

America has tried to dispatch God from our knowledge. It doesn't matter that politicians still like to use the phrase "God bless America" to conclude their speeches. The reality that God is absent from their programs and ideas, that His word is ignored on all moral areas of their agendas makes their use of that phrase nothing more than a violation of the Third Commandment found in Exodus 20:7, *"You shall not take the name of the LORD your God in vain, for the LORD will not hold him guiltless who takes His name in vain."* One meaning of vanity is "with empty meaning." That would apply to much of what is said today in the name of God. Dispatching God from our mind is the first charge made against man in Romans 1:28.

The result of the act of forgetting God is a litany of unrighteousness. The first acts of unrighteousness Paul has already covered in Romans 1:26 and 27. Here was given the divine denouncement of acts of homosexual and lesbian behavior. These were not empty words. God did not make an empty comment when declaring the great sin of homosexuality.

He said that it was a defiance of His nature and His glory for men and women to indulge in such conduct. God here makes a solemn declaration to man – It is impossible for a person to say that they believe God is true and still engage without shame in homosexual acts. If God is true, then His word is true. We cannot know God in His fullness without His word. If we reject His word then we are merely worshipping a different God who cannot hear, save or care about us. It is with this first and profound condemnation of homosexuality that God begins His litany of man's sins.

Next God declares that man is filled with unrighteousness. Man must come to the full understanding of this truth that gripped St. Augustine's heart and lead Him to Christ. He read this in Romans 13:14, *"But put on the Lord Jesus Christ, and make no provision for the flesh, to fulfill its lusts."* He fully knew the flesh. He knew it personally and he knew that what Paul said in Romans 7:18 was true. *"For I know that in me (that is, in my flesh,) dwelleth no good thing."* To say that one is righteous and good in the sin they are committing and therefore that they cannot be displeasing to God because "we were made in His image" is a falsehood fed to us by the father of lies, the devil.

Immediately the Scripture returns in this indictment to the very sins of Canaan – immorality! God had taken Israel as His own wife. This is pictured in the book of Hosea very clearly. The whole nation had become an adulteress against Him. He had an indictment against them He told them in chapter 4. The first indictment was that they had forgotten the knowledge of Him. (Vs. 1 & 6) Compare that to Paul's indictment in Romans 1:21-23. Followed by this was their list of sins. Prominently is found immorality. Again compare this to Romans 1:24-27. They had played the harlot in choosing false gods to obey. The result was that they also gave themselves over to physical depravity and ever sexual immorality. Playing the harlot with human theologies is as much an act of immorality as physical immorality would be. Choosing to love the words and ideas of man more than the words and ideas of God is immorality of the spirit. The visible church today is playing with spiritual immorality while the world runs rampant with physical immorality.

The list of sins in God's indictment of man goes on and on in Romans 1. They cover every emotional, physical, familial and spiritual aspect of our lives. The crowning statement, however, is found in verse 32. *"Who, knowing the righteous judgment of God, that those who practice such things are deserving of death, not only do the same but also approve of those who practice them."* We are not ignorant of how much we hate this list of sins in other people. We know that justice will be served when many of these offenses are punished by death in human courts. We would also say, in relation to others but not ourselves, that people who do such things have no place in heaven. Years ago I read a study, and I don't remember where, that was conducted in prisons. No matter how serious the crime was that each had committed, all knew or believed that others were worse than them. They readily saw that others deserved punishment for their crimes even if they didn't deserve their own. How utterly like us all!

We know that judgment is right – at least for others. We know that judgment is just. We collectively believe that God will somehow bring about judgment. We just don't believe that He is in any hurry to do so or to do so to us in particular. And so we tend to exempt ourselves from judgment. A pastor I know, who lives in New York City, was asked to do a funeral. He had never met the departed. He gave a straightforward message about God's care for man and His grace to those who would believe. He said nothing derogatory about the deceased in any way. The family was very upset. "Why," they asked, "didn't you put him in heaven in your sermon?" Of course they never asked the question to him, they just passed their anger along through the funeral director. The attitude was simple; he wasn't so bad, shouldn't he be in heaven? Judgment is for the other fellow, and that is how mankind, in their rejection of God, believes.

But God's indictment continues. Not only are the practitioners of these sins going to face judgment, so are those who take pleasure in them. Sexual immorality and violence dominate the TV airwaves. These items are on the list of God's righteous judgment. Those who do them will be judged. What about those who vicariously enjoy them? God says that judgment passes on to them as well.

Sexual immorality, whether it is fornication, adultery, pornography or homosexuality is against the law of God. The actors who portray the characters engaged in the activity take financial pleasure from their roles. The writers and producers of these shows take pleasure in creating and producing them. The advertisers take pleasure in promoting them. The public takes pleasure in watching them. God will judge. He will judge each of the parties. The politician who says that sexual immorality is OK will be judged. The people who support that politician's policies will be judged. God will judge all of these who are without the church.

The church that upholds the practice of sexual immorality will be judged. Churches aren't buildings. Churches are people. People must OK or sign-off on impurity for it to take effect. People must either turn a blind eye to sin or openly endorse sin for sin to take root in the church. Either way the outcome is that they took enough pleasure in the anticipated gains of this sin that they let it move forward. "Our numbers are shrinking. We must attract new people." That is the common statement made today by those who don't want to make waves. "There is really nothing wrong with that behavior. It is simply some archaic laws that say so." That is the statement made by those who willingly teach error. Either way a pleasurable goal is set forth as the reasoning for stepping deeper into the cesspool of sin. For either reason the judgment of God is righteous and just.

Should the church doors be shut to the sexually immoral? No. The church door should be wide open to them so they can hear of both the grace and judgment of God who loved us so that He gave His only Son for our sins. But, the church is not open to their membership until they repent and come to Christ. The sacraments/ordinances of the church are not open to them until they repent and come to Christ. Leadership in the church is certainly not open to them until they repent and come to Christ. God has a righteous indictment against the sins of man. He will judge certainly and in the way He chooses. In the church we are to take this seriously. We are to love Him and respect His judgments. We are to live out our lives as His holy bride.

CHAPTER TWENTY-ONE

THE CHURCH'S GREATEST COMMODITY

What is it that the church offers to each community and to the world as a whole? What "product" do we have that makes people want to buy at "our store"? Is our product social acceptability? Is our product cultural accommodation? Is our product to be one that simply pleases the world with its candy-coated innocuousness? These are questions that the church has begun to ask itself in greater measure over the past 50 years? Why are we here? Mr. Thomas says our commodity is moral authority[1]. Is he right?

The Scriptures record that Jesus had authority. The people were astounded at His message because He spoke with authority. Matthew 7:28-29 says, *"And so it was, when Jesus had ended these sayings, that the people were astonished at His teaching, for He taught them as one having authority, and not as the scribes."* Again in Luke 4, in another place and situation, the people made the same comment. Luke 4:36: *"Then they were all amazed and spoke among themselves, saying, 'What a word this is! For with authority and power **He commands** the unclean spirits, and they come out'."* Jesus' authority came from who He was, the very Son of God. He wasn't questioning whether He was right or not. He spoke what the Father told Him to speak as He declared in John 8:28, *"I do* *nothing of Myself; but as My Father taught Me, I speak these things."* The authority of the Son came from the Father's own teaching.

The church's authority comes from the same God. It comes from the same words of God that Jesus, God the Son, spoke Himself. It is not a moral authority based on a contemporary view of man. It is not riddled with argument and dissenting opinions as was the wisdom of the Scribes. It is not temporized by circumstance or the "movement of the moment". It is based on the solid rock of God Himself who changes not. Malachi 3:6 states, *"For I am the LORD, I do not change."* This great declaration of God should make the church stand up and take notice. The God who does not change has a word that is eternally correct and that is our authority.

More precisely, the God who gave the word is our authority. Any teaching or positions of men's ideas that contradict the eternal word of God are a violation of His authority. Yes, that authority is moral because God is moral. It is also absolute because God is absolute. It is final because God is the first and the last. His say was first to be spoken and He will have the last say. The last things He has to say will not contradict the first things He had to say because He changes not. That is authority of all times, places, situations and human speculations.

Jesus spoke with authority because He spoke the words of God. The church is to speak with authority because the church is to speak the words of God. When the church stops speaking the words of God, as Mr. Thomas asks us to do, the church will lose authority. If we change the message from the one that He gave us, we have nothing to contribute to the real welfare of men. We may feed the hungry and clothe the naked and visit those in prison, but if we do not bring them the word of God they will still perish and what have we benefitted them? The authority is in the word. Jesus became the Living Word and demonstrated the authority of God.

When Jesus became the Living Word, leaving the glory of heaven to dwell among us, did He strive to be pleasing to men?

If we take some Scriptures out of context we might think that the answer is yes. He was certainly a popular man at different times in His ministry. In John chapter 6 Jesus fed the 5000 men plus women and children. The next day those same people were hungry again and went looking for Him. Had he pleased them? Yes, He had. Did He please them the next day? No, He did not. That day He preached them a sermon which begins in John 6:36 and continues to John 6:59. That sermon did not please them. In John 6:66 we have a very sad verse. *"From that time many of His disciples went back and walked with Him no more."* He turned out to not be such a crowd pleaser after all. He wasn't building a movement based on the number of His followers but on the truth of God.

Jesus could have picked a political party in Israel to align Himself with and increased His popular acceptance. There were three major parties. There were the liberals who were called Sadducees. They didn't believe in the spirit realm. They were the largest of the political parties. Then there were the Pharisees. They were true conservatives. They were the letter of the law type of folks. Unfortunately they mostly believed the letter of the law applied to others more than themselves. Then there were the Herodians. They were the get along with Rome group. This group could have gotten Jesus some quality press time in the empire's capital city. Matthew chapters 21 through 23 give us Jesus' response to these groups. He certainly wasn't trying to make Himself Mr. Popularity. He told them they were all wrong and that God was right. The very issue of authority even came up. He asserted God's authority. They were left speechless.

That is how it will be at the end of the age as well. All the people who squawk today about how Jesus didn't mean what He said; all the people who mock the truth of God's word as it is delivered to us; all of those who believe that they should be God's editors will one day stand before the great throne of Him who is raised from the dead. When He comes to judge the quick and the dead and they see the glory of His throne and the true power of His might and as He pronounces upon them their final doom, they shall be speechless - except to say, "Jesus Christ is Lord."

No, Jesus Christ did not come to win any popularity contests. He came, as it says in Luke 19:10, *"to seek and to save that which was lost."* In what way was it lost? It was lost in sin. What was lost? All men were lost. Jesus came to save us from God's just judgment. He didn't come to be popular. He came to tell us the truth and the truth is seldom popular. It is not popular with those who wish to live in their own immoral lifestyle choices. It is not popular with those who want to simply live in their own self-directed lifestyle choices. It is not popular with those who believe they are wiser than God. But it is still truth and it is still upheld by Christ.

Jesus understood the true nature about how most people really felt about Him. He told His disciples in John 15:18 that the world hated Him. *"If the world hates you, you know that it hated Me before it hated you."* Jesus wasn't conned by temporary popularity or acceptance. He knew that they hated Him because He spoke for God. He went on to say in John 15:23 that they just didn't hate Him but that they also hated His Father, *"He who hates Me hates My Father also."* And why did they hate Him, because with authority He exposed the darkness of their sin and men loved darkness and hated the light. Jesus is the Light of the World. *"And this is the condemnation, that the light has come into the world, and men loved darkness rather than light, because their deeds were evil. For everyone practicing evil* **_hates the light_** *and does not come to the light, lest his deeds should be exposed."* (John 3:19-21)

How is this hatred expressed? In 1989 homosexual activists stormed St. Patrick's Cathedral in New York City, disrupted Mass and spit on the Eucharist (the communion bread). The liberal movie maker Michael Moore praised the action[2]. In 2008 "A homosexual activist group disrupted Sunday services at a Michigan Assemblies of God-affiliated church, throwing fliers, shouting slogans at churchgoers, and kissing each other.[3]" In

Brazil homosexuals held a "kiss in" on the steps of a Catholic church during Mass[4]. But it is not only in disrupting the services of the church that homosexuals demonstrate their true hatred for God the Father, Christ the Son and His church.

They don't want to just invade it to disrupt, they also want to invade the leadership of the church to teach the error that their practice is OK with God. Their progress in this quest is seen by the capitulation of several denominations to having ordained clergy who are homosexuals and opening the Eucharist/communion table to practicing homosexuals. In addition they have taken the rite of holy matrimony, divinely ordained between a man and a woman, and claimed that it is a moral right for homosexuals to also call themselves "married". They have fulfilled the warning of Jude 4, *"For certain men have crept in unnoticed, who long ago were marked out for this condemnation, ungodly men, who turn the grace of our God into lewdness and deny the only Lord God and our Lord Jesus Christ."* Jude's warning continues in verses 17-19. *"But you, beloved, remember the words which were spoken before by the apostles of our Lord Jesus Christ: how they told you that there would be mockers in the last time who would walk according to their own ungodly lusts. These are sensual persons, who cause divisions, not having the spirit."*

Notice that Jude connects the rejection of Christ with the rejection of God because there is no spiritual life, no Holy Spirit, in the false teachers. There is no fear of the great triune God before their eyes. They desire to destroy the church from within. They deny Him by saying that what He said is not true. They try to destroy the authority of His word. They turn the glorious gospel of redemption into a message of lewdness and personal freedom. They seek to destroy the church's greatest commodity, the truth of the word of God. If God's word is not true, then all men are free to choose to live and do as they please. They are free, as Paul said, to hold to a form of godliness while denying the power thereof. (II Timothy 3:5) But that freedom will end at death. Then the certain law of God takes over. From such as these Paul warns us to turn away.

The church is not supposed to embrace such error. The church is to reject it and to turn away its ears from hearing such error. The church is to recognize that these men, as Jude said, are already marked by God for condemnation, and to get away from their tents as Moses warned the people of Israel to get away from the tents of Dathan and Abiram. Moses said to them, *"Depart now from the tents of these wicked men! Touch nothing of theirs, lest you be consumed in all their sins."* (Numbers 16:26)

The apostle Paul has enjoined the church to be separate from the world and its sinful teachings. He asks in II Corinthians 6:15-16, *"And what accord has Christ with Belial? Or what part has a believer with an unbeliever? And what agreement has the temple of God with idols?"* It was the idolatry of Canaan that fed the total moral corruption of the land. It is the idolatry of self that proclaims that "my sin is not sin if it brings me fulfillment and satisfaction". It is the idolatry of self that proclaims, "I have greater wisdom and understanding than God." It is the same old idolatry of Canaan that permeates its stench in the holy church of God today. After Paul asked the church the rhetorical question of how we can have accord with Belial, he concludes the passage with this admonition. *"Therefore, 'Come out from among them and be separate, says the Lord. Do not touch what is unclean, and I will receive you'."* II Cor. 6:17

To maintain the integrity of the church; to maintain the one true commodity that we have – the everlasting and true Word of God, the true church needs to declare a separation of itself from the horrible idolatry of Canaan. True believers must come out from denominations that have grown perverse in teaching and practice. The true church needs to uphold the truth of the Word as inviolate and maintain the teaching given to it by God alone. The true church needs to be true to the one true message delivered by God to man. That message is the authority that changes lives, gives hope, grants salvation. That authority is our one true commodity. Without that we have nothing to offer.

We began this book with the word and we end with the word. The word of God is true and everlasting. It is our message, our commodity, our power and our hope. *"Forever, O Lord, Thy word is settled in heaven."* (Ps. 119:89) Amen and amen.

BIBLIOGRAPHY

Chapter 1:
Chapter 2:
Chapter 3:

1. Presbyterian Church (U.S.A.). (n.d.). Retrieved from http://www.pcusa.org/
2. The Domestic and Foreign Missionary Society of the Protestant Episcopal Church in the United States of America. (n.d.). Retrieved from http://www.episcopalchurch.org/
3. Evangelical Lutheran Church in America. (n.d.). Retrieved from http://www.elca.org/
4. United Church of Christ. (n.d.). Retrieved from http://www.ucc.org/
5. Reformed Church in America. (n.d.). Retrieved from https://www.rca.org/
6. DeYoung, K. (2010, January). *Perspectives: Essay: Why Not Belhar?* Retrieved from Reformed Church in America: http://www.rca.org/page.aspx?pid=6245
7. Sandnes, H. E. (2008, October 22). *Our Mother in Heaven.* Retrieved from KILDEN: http://eng.kilden.forskningsradet.no/c52778/nyhet/vis.html?tid=54978
8. Thomas, O. (2006, November 19). *When religion loses its credibility.* Retrieved from USA TODAY:

http://usatoday30.usatoday.com/news/opinion/edit
orials/2006-11-19-forum-religion_x.htm

Chapter 4:

1. Ibid.

Chapter 5:

1. First Amendment Center. (n.d.). Retrieved from
   http://www.firstamendmentcenter.org/

2. Thomas, O. (2006, November 19). *When religion loses its
   credibility.* Retrieved from USA TODAY:
   http://usatoday30.usatoday.com/news/opinion/edit
   orials/2006-11-19-forum-religion_x.htm

Chapter 6:

1. Ibid.

2. Landsberg, M. (2010, September 28). *Atheists, agnostics
   most knowledgeable about religion, survey says.* Retrieved
   from Los Angeles Times:
   http://articles.latimes.com/2010/sep/28/nation/la-
   na-religion-survey-20100928

3. Gallup, A., & Simmons, W. W. (2000, October 20).
   Six in Ten Americans Read Bible at Least Occasionally.
   Retrieved from Gallup, Inc.:
   http://www.gallup.com/poll/2416/six-ten-
   americans-read-bible-least-occasionally.aspx

4. The Gale Group, Inc. (2008). *West's Encyclopedia of
   American Law, edition 2.* Retrieved from The Free
   Online Law Dictionary: http://legal-
   dictionary.thefreedictionary.com/sodomy

Chapter 7:

Chapter 8:

1. Thomas, O. (2006, November 19). *When religion loses its
   credibility.* Retrieved from USA TODAY:
   http://usatoday30.usatoday.com/news/opinion/edit
   orials/2006-11-19-forum-religion_x.htm

Chapter 9:

Chapter 10:

1. Moloch. (n.d.). In *Wikipedia*. Retrieved from http://en.wikipedia.org/wiki/Moloch
2. Quartz Hill School of Theology. (n.d.). *The Religion of the Canaanites*. Retrieved from http://www.theology.edu/canaan.htm
3. Ibid.
4. Fletcher, E. (n.d.). *Gods and Goddesses, the Golden Calf, fertility religions, bestiality*. Retrieved from Bible Cities and Holy Lands: http://www.bible-lands.net/cities/dan/450-fertility-religions-the-golden-calf

Chapter 11:
1. Thomas, O. (2006, November 19). *When religion loses its credibility*. Retrieved from USA TODAY: http://usatoday30.usatoday.com/news/opinion/editorials/2006-11-19-forum-religion_x.htm
2. Centers for Disease Control and Prevention. (n.d.). *FASTSTATS - Unmarried Childbearing*. Retrieved from http://www.cdc.gov/nchs/fastats/unmarry.htm
3. Thomas, O. (2006, November 19). *When religion loses its credibility*. Retrieved from USA TODAY: http://usatoday30.usatoday.com/news/opinion/editorials/2006-11-19-forum-religion_x.htm

Chapter 12:
Chapter 13:
Chapter 14:
Chapter 15:
1. Gallup, A., & Simmons, W. W. (2000, October 20). *Six in Ten Americans Read Bible at Least Occasionally*. Retrieved from Gallup, Inc.: http://www.gallup.com/poll/2416/six-ten-americans-read-bible-least-occasionally.aspx
2. The Christian Broadcasting Network, Inc. (2009, July 24). *Know Your Bible? Many Christians Don't*. Retrieved from

http://www.cbn.com/cbnnews/us/2009/June/Do-You-Know-Your-Bible-Many-Christians-Dont/

3. Barna Research Ltd. (2011, July 26). *Barna Examines Trends in 14 Religious Factors over 20 Years (1991 to 2011)*. Retrieved from https://www.barna.org/faith-spirituality/504-barna-examines-trends-in-14-religious-factors-over-20-years-1991-to-2011

4. Newport, F. (2004, March 23). *A Look at Americans and Religion Today*. Retrieved from Gallup, Inc.: http://www.gallup.com/poll/11089/Look-Americans-Religion-Today.aspx

5. Ontario Consultants on Religious Tolerance. (2007, August 10). *How many North Americans go regularly to church?* Retrieved from http://www.religioustolerance.org/rel_rate.htm

6. Harris Interactive Inc. (2006, December 20). *Religious Views and Beliefs Vary Greatly by Country, According to the Latest Financial Times/Harris Poll*. Retrieved from http://www.harrisinteractive.com/NEWS/allnewsbydate.asp?NewsID=1130

7. Vine, W. E., Unger, M. F., & White, W. (1996). *Vine's Complete Expository Dictionary of Old and New Testament Words*. Nashville, TN: Thomas Nelson, Inc.

Chapter 16:

1. Thomas, O. (2006, November 19). *When religion loses its credibility*. Retrieved from USA TODAY: http://usatoday30.usatoday.com/news/opinion/editorials/2006-11-19-forum-religion_x.htm

Chapter 17:

1. Genung, M. (2005, June 17). *How Many Porn Addicts are in Your Church?* Retrieved from Crosswalk.com: http://www.crosswalk.com/church/pastors-or-leadership/how-many-porn-addicts-are-in-your-church-1336107.html

2. Merriam-Webster, Incorporated. (2007). *Merriam-*

Webster's Collegiate Dictionary, Eleventh Edition. Springfield, Massachusetts, USA: Merriam-Webster, Incorporated.

3. BBC NEWS. (2006, February 21). *Births out of wedlock 'pass 40%'.* Retrieved from http://news.bbc.co.uk/2/hi/uk_news/4733330.stm

4. Child Trends. (2012, November). *Births to Unmarried Women.* Retrieved from http://www.childtrends.org/?indicators=births-to-unmarried-women

5. Divercestatistics.org. (n.d.). *Information on Divorce Rate Statistics.* Retrieved from http://www.divorcestatistics.org/

Chapter 18:

Chapter 19:

Chapter 20:

Chapter 21:

1. Thomas, O. (2006, November 19). *When religion loses its credibility.* Retrieved from USA TODAY: http://usatoday30.usatoday.com/news/opinion/editorials/2006-11-19-forum-religion_x.htm

2. Catholic League. (2013, January 10). *MICHAEL MOORE LIKES CHURCH INVASIONS.* Retrieved from http://www.catholicleague.org/michael-moore-likes-church-invasions/

3. Eternal Word Television Network, Inc. (2008, November 13). *Gay Activists Disrupt Sunday Service at Michigan Church.* Retrieved from http://www.ewtn.com/vnews/getstory.asp?number=92179

4. National Organization for Marriage. (2011, May 17). *Gay Activists Stage "Kiss In" During Mass after Brazil High Court OKs Civil Unions.* Retrieved from https://www.nomblog.com/8679

Made in the USA
Charleston, SC
07 July 2013